Summer Fit™

Let's Get Ready for Eighth Grade!

Summer Fit Seventh to Eighth Grade

Author: Veronica Brand

Fitness and Nutrition: Lisa Roberts RN, BSN, PHN, James Cordova, Charles Miller, Steve Edwards, Missy Jones, Barbara Sherwood, John Bartlette, Malu Egido, Michael Ward

Healthy Family Lifestyle: Jay and Jen Jacobs & Marci and Courtney Crozier

Layout and Design: Scott Aucutt

Cover Design and Illustrations: Andy Carlson

Illustrations: Roxanne Ottley and Scott Aucutt

Series Created by George Starks

Summer Fit Dedication

Summer Fit is dedicated to Julia Hobbs and Carla Fisher who are the authors and unsung heroes of the original summer workbook series that helped establish the importance of summer learning. These women helped pioneer summer learning and dedicated their lives to teaching children and supporting parents. Carla and Julia made the world a better place by touching the lives of others using their love of education.

Summer Fit is also dedicated to Michael Starks whose presence is missed dearly, but who continues to teach us every day the importance of having courage in difficult times and treating others with respect, dignity, and a genuine concern for others.

Summer Fit Caution

If you have any questions regarding your child's ability to complete any of the suggested fitness activities consult your family doctor or child's pediatrician. Some of these exercises may require adult supervision. Children should stretch and warm up before exercises. Do not push children past their comfort level or ability. These physical fitness activities were created to be fun for parents and caregivers as well as the child, but not as a professional training or weight loss program. Exercise should stop immediately if you or your child experiences any of the following symptoms: pain, feeling dizzy or faint, nausea, or severe fatigue.

Printed in the USA
All Rights Reserved
ISBN: 978-0-9853526-1-5
www.SummerFitLearning.com

TABLE OF CONTENTS

Parent Section

Activities and Exercises

Extras

Dear Parents,

Without opportunities to learn and practice essential skills over the summer months, most children fall behind academically. Research shows that summer learning loss varies, but that children can lose the equivalency of 2.5 months of math and 2 months of reading skills while away from school. In addition, children lose more than just academic knowledge during the summer. Research also shows that children are at greater risk of actually gaining more weight during summer vacation than during the school year:

FACT 1 — All young people experience learning losses when they do not engage in educational activities during the summer. Research spanning 100 years shows that students typically score lower on standardized tests at the end of summer vacation than they do on the same tests at the beginning of the summer (White, 1906; Heyns, 1978; Entwisle & Alexander 1992; Cooper, 1996; Downey et al, 2004).

FACT 2 — Research shows that children gain weight three times faster during the summer months – gaining as much weight during the summer as they do during the entire school year – even though the summertime is three times shorter. Von Hippel, P. T., Powell, B., Downey, D.B., & Rowland, N. (2007).

FACT 3 — In the New York City school system, elementary and middle school students who placed in the top third of a fitness scale had better math and reading scores than students in the bottom third of the fitness scale. Those who were in the top 5% for fitness scored an average of 36 percentage points higher on state reading and math exams than did the least-fit 5%. New York City Department of Health. (2009)

Summer vacation is a great opportunity to use a variety of resources and programs to extend the academic learning experience and to reinforce life and social skills. It is an opportunity to give learning a different look and feel than what children are used to during the school year. Summer is a season that should be fun and carefree, but do not underestimate the opportunity and importance of helping children prepare for the upcoming school year. The key to a successful new school year is keeping your children active and learning this summer!

Sincerely,

Summer Fit Learning

FACT
You are your
child's greatest
teacher.

Inside Summer Fit

Purpose

The purpose of Summer Fit is to offer a comprehensive program for parents that promotes health and physical activity along side of academic and social skills. Summer Fit is designed to help create healthy and balanced family lifestyles.

Stay Smart

Summer Fit contains activities in reading, writing, math, language arts, science, geography and technology.

Program Components

Summer Fit activities and exercises are divided into 10 sections to correlate with the traditional 10 weeks of summer. Each section begins with a weekly overview and incentive calendar so parents and children can talk about the week ahead while reviewing the previous week. There are 10 pages of activities for each week. The child does 2 pages a day that should take 20-30 minutes a day to complete. Each day offers a simple routine to reinforce basic skills and includes a physical fitness exercise and healthy habit. Each week also reinforces a core value on a daily basis to build character and social skills. Activities start off easy and progressively get more difficult so by the end of the workbook children are mentally, physically and socially prepared for the grade ahead.

Stay Cool

Summer Fit uses core value activities, facts and role models to reinforce the importance of good character and social skills.

Stay Active

Summer Fit uses a daily fitness exercise and wellness tips to keep children moving and having fun.

Summer Fit includes a daily exercise program that children complete as part of their one-page of activities a day. These daily exercises and movement activities foster active lifestyles and get parents and children moving together.

Summer Fit uses daily value-based activities to reinforce good behavior.

Summer Fit promotes the body-brain connection and gives parents the tools to motivate children to use both.

Summer Fit includes an online component that gives children and parents additional summer learning and fitness resources at SummerFitLearning.com.

Summer Fit contains activities and exercises created by educators, parents and trainers committed to creating active learning environments that include movement and play as part of the learning experience.

Summer Fit uses role models from around the world to introduce and reinforce core values and the importance of good behavior.

The Whole Child philosophy is based on the belief that every child should be healthy, engaged, supported and challenged in all aspects of their lives. Investing in the *overall* development of your child is critical to their personal health and well being. There is increased awareness that a balanced approach to nurturing and teaching our children will benefit all aspects of their lives; therefore creating well rounded students who are better equipped to successfully navigate the ups and downs of their education careers.

Supports Common Core Standards

The Common Core provides teachers and parents with a common understanding of what students are expected to learn. These standards will provide appropriate benchmarks for all students, regardless of where they live and be applied for students in grades K-12. Summer Fit is aligned to Common Core Standards.

Learn more at: CoreStandards.org

Top 5 Parent Summer Tips

1 **Routine:** Set a time and a place for your child to complete their activities and exercises each day.

2 **Balance:** Use a combination of resources to reinforce classroom skills in fun ways.

3 **Motivate and Encourage:** Inspire your child to complete their daily activities and exercises. Get excited and show your support of their accomplishments!

4 **Play as a Family:** Slap "high 5," jump up and down and get silly! Show how fun it is to be active by doing it yourself! Health Experts recommend 60 minutes of play a day and kids love seeing parents playing and having fun!

5 **Eat Healthy (and together):** Kids are more likely to eat less healthy during the summer, than during the school year. Put food back on the table and eat together at least once a day.

Jay Jacobs
Former contestant
of NBC's
The Biggest Loser

Physical activity is critical to your child's health and well-being. Research shows that children with better health are in school more days, learn better, have higher self esteem and lower risk of developing chronic diseases.

Exercise Provides:

✔ Stronger muscles and bones

✔ Leaner body because exercise helps control body fat

✔ Increased blood flow to the brain and wellness at home

✔ Lower blood pressure and blood cholesterol levels

✔ Kids who are active are less likely to develop weight issues, display more self-confidence, perform better academically and enjoy a better overall quality of life!

Jay Jacobs lost 181 pounds on Season 11 of NBC's *The Biggest Loser*.

Sedentary lifestyles, weight issues and unhealthy habits need to be addressed at home. It is more likely that your child will include healthy habits as part of their everyday life if they understand:

✔ Why staying active and eating healthy is important

✔ What are healthy habits and what are not

✔ How to be healthy, active and happy

Go to the Health and Wellness Index in the back of the book for more Family Health and Wellness Tips.

Warm Up!

It is always best to prepare your body for any physical activity by moving around and stretching.

Get Loose! Stretch!

Move your head from side to side, trying to touch each shoulder. Now move your head forward, touching your chin to your chest and then looking up and back as far as you can, trying to touch your back with the back of your head.

Touch your toes when standing, bend over at the waist and touch the end of your toes or the floor. Hold this for 10 seconds.

Get Moving

Walk or jog for 3-5 minutes to warm up before you exercise. Shake your arms and roll your shoulders when you are finished walking or jogging.

A healthy diet and daily exercise will maximize the likelihood of children growing up healthy and strong. Children are still growing and adding bone mass, so a balanced diet is very important to their overall health. Provide three nutritious meals a day that include fruits and vegetables. Try to limit fast food consumption, and find time to cook more at home where you know the source of your food and how your food is prepared. Provide your child with healthy, well-portioned snacks, and try to keep them from eating too much at a time.

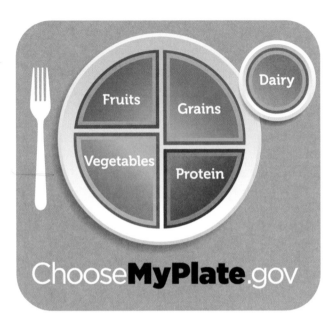

SCORE! A HEALTHY EATING GOAL

As a rule of thumb, avoid foods and drinks that are high in sugars, fat, or caffeine. Try to provide fruits, vegetables, grains, lean meats, chicken, fish, and low-fat dairy products as part of a healthy meal when possible. Obesity and being overweight, even in children, can significantly increase the risk of heart disease, diabetes, and other chronic illnesses. Creating an active lifestyle this summer that includes healthy eating and exercise will help your child maintain a healthy weight and protect them from certain illnesses throughout the year.

Let's Eat Healthy!

5 Steps to Improve Eating Habits of Your Family

1) Make fresh fruits and veggies readily available.
2) Cook more at home, and sit down for dinner as a family.
3) Limit consumption of soda, desserts and sugary cereals.
4) Serve smaller portions.
5) Limit snacks to just one or two daily.

Integrating more technology into your middle school students learning experience will allow your child to expand and use their knowledge exponentially. Technology is an important and natural next step in the learning process. It helps simulate real world experiences, allows them to interact with other learners and gives them the opportunity to access and work with information from around the world.

Encourage your child to use technology for more then social and entertainment purposes. Remind them that it is a learning tool as well. Technology gives them the opportunity to apply their mastery of basic skills and fundamentals in reading, writing, math and language arts in creative, fun and purposeful ways. It is a "next step" that is grounded in their ability to be an independent learner.

It is important to move forward with a balanced and mindful approach in order to avoid a sedentary lifestyle. Continue to put limits on screen time and encourage outside play and face-to-face friendships as part of a healthy and balanced household.

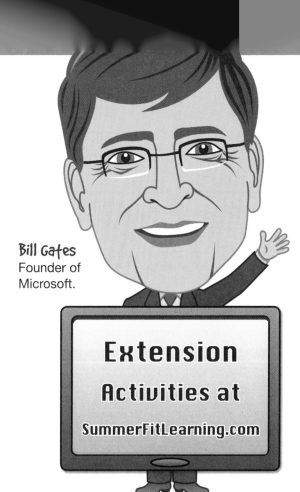

Bill Gates
Founder of Microsoft.

Extension Activities at
SummerFitLearning.com

KEYS TO TECH SUCCESS

1 Explore different technology resources and products with your child.

2 Utilize technology as a teaching tool to help extend and enhance their overall learning experience.

3 Develop learning activities that incorporate the utilization of technology. Show your child that technology is more then gaming and social networks.

4 Enforce responsible, ethical and legal use of technology.

Understanding core values allows your child to have a clearer understanding of their own behavior in your home, in their classroom and in our communities. Core values are fundamental to society and are incorporated into our civil laws, but are taught first and foremost at home. Parents and guardians are the most important and influential people in a child's life. It is up to you to raise children who respect and accept themselves, and others around them.

Role Models

A role model is a person who serves as an example of a particular value or trait. Though it seems difficult to find positive role models, there are many people today, and throughout history who have exemplified in their own actions the values that we strive to have ourselves and teach our children.

Elanore Roosevelt

First lady of the USA and an activist for the poor, woman's rights, children's causes, racial equality, and human rights.

Pelé

Regarded by many as the best soccer player to ever play the game.

Kristi Yamaguchi

In 1992, she became the first American woman to win an Olympic gold medal in figure skating since 1976.

Bullying

In recent years, bullying has become a leading topic of concern. It is a complex issue, and can be difficult for parents to know what to do when they hear that their child is being bullied or is bullying others. Bullying is always wrong. It is critical that you intervene appropriately when bullying occurs. Make sure your child understands what bullying means. Check in with your child often to make sure he/she knows you are interested and aware of what is going on in their social lives.

Learn more at StopBullying.gov

Books Build Better Brains!

Reading is considered the gateway to all learning, so it is critical as a parent or caregiver to assist and encourage children to read at all grade levels regardless of reading ability.

1. Create a daily reading routine. A reading routine provides the practice a child needs to reinforce and build reading and literacy skills.

2. Create a summer reading list. Choose a variety of books, including fairy tales, poems, fiction and non-fiction books.

3. Start a family summer reading club.

4. Discuss with your child a book that you are reading. Show your child how much you enjoy reading and ask them to discuss some of their favorite books.

5. Combine summer movies with summer reading. Read the book before going to see this summer's blockbuster. If the book is not available, find a similar topic.

 Read 30 minutes a day!

CYBER READERS: Books in a Digital World

With the increasing amount of digital content that is available, it is easy to access information and media on the go or at home. Currently, there are numerous studies researching how e-content is impacting how information is being retained and how it impacts classroom performance. It seems there are advantages for both e-content and traditional print, so it is important to cultivate a reading friendly environment that encourages and accepts both. More studies will likely show that there is material suited for learning in a digital format, as well as lessons that best remain in traditional textbooks.

Find these books at the library, bookstore or online. Summer is as much a time to read for enjoyment, as it is to maintain reading skills while you are away from school. We recommend you read for a minimum of 30 minutes a day during the summer - Happy Reading!

Something to Declare
By Alvarez, Julia

Tuck Everlasting
By Babbitt, Natalie

My Brother Sam Is Dead
By Collier, James and Christopher

With Every Drop of Blood
By Collier, James and Christopher

Out of Time
By Cooney, Caroline

Red Kayak
By Cummings, Priscilla

Mockingbird
By Erskine, Kathryn

Johnny Tremain
By Forbes, Esther

Games
By Gorman, Carol

House of Dies Drear
By Hamilton, Virginia

Hiroshima
By Hersey, John

Farewell to Manzanar
By Houston, Jeanne and James

Call of the Wild
By London, Jack

The Sea Wolf
By London, Jack

A Night to Remember
By Lord, Walter

Silent Storm
By Macy, Anne Sullivan

Dog Friday
By McKay, Hilary

The Glory Field
By Myers, Walter Dean

Sarah Bishop
By O'Dell, Scott

Lyddie
By Paterson, Katharine

Park's Quest
By Paterson, Katharine

Life As We Knew It
By Pfeffer, Susan Beth

Cast Two Shadows
By Rinaldi, Ann

Moon Dancer
By Rotkowski, Margaret

The Van Gogh Cafe
By Rylant, Cynthia

All-of-a-Kind Family
By Taylor, Sydney

The Bomb
By Taylor, Theodore

By Wartski, Maureen Crane
A Boat To Nowhere
By Taylor, Theodore

Dragonwings
By Yep, Laurence

When I Was Your Age: Original Stories About Growing Up
By Yep, Laurence

Skills Assessment Grade 7 - Math

1.
    0.49
    1.86
  + 32.1
———

2.
    43.69
   - 6.325
———

3.
    93
  x 8.6
———

4. $762.34 - 12.8 =$ _____

5. $8.4 \times 9.1 =$ _____

6. $2.1\ \overline{1\ 7\ 2.2}$

7. $27\ \overline{4\ 2.1\ 2}$

8. $308 \div 3.5 =$ _____

9. $\dfrac{8}{9} + \dfrac{2}{3} =$

10. $\dfrac{8}{9} - \dfrac{2}{3} =$

11. $\dfrac{8}{9} \times \dfrac{2}{3} =$

12. $\dfrac{8}{9} \div \dfrac{2}{3} =$

13. $3\dfrac{1}{3} + 2\dfrac{1}{6} =$

14. $3\dfrac{1}{3} - 2\dfrac{1}{6} =$

15. $3\dfrac{1}{3} \times 2\dfrac{1}{6} =$

16. $3\dfrac{1}{3} \div 2\dfrac{1}{6} =$

17. $\dfrac{9}{15} = \dfrac{x}{5}$

18. $\dfrac{37}{100} =$ _____ %

19. $36\% = \dfrac{9}{n}$

20. $0.81 =$ _____ %

21. $0.8 = \dfrac{4}{n}$

22. $-3 + (-6) =$ _____

23. $6 + (-7) =$ _____

24. $8 + (-3) =$ _____

25. $-3 + 6 =$ _____

26. $-2 - 6 =$ _____

27. $-8 - (-10) =$ _____

28. $-3 \times (-5) =$ _____

29. $-2 \times 7 =$ _____

30. $-8 \times 6 =$ _____

31. $5 \times 3 =$ _____

32. $45 \div (-9) =$ _____

33. $-35 \div 5 =$ _____

34. $-56 \div 7 =$ _____

35. $-28 \div (-2) =$ _____

36. $-4x > 16$ _____

37. $x + 4 > 2$ _____

38. $x - 1 > 5$ _____

39. $2y + 7 < 15$ _____

40. $-39 \div x = -3$ _____

41. $56 = -4x$ _____

42. $5z + 22 = 8z + 16$ _____

43. $4a + 17 = 2a + 21$ _____

44. $3t - 14 = 18 - t$ _____

45. $63 - a = 5a + 27$ _____

Match the following genres of literature with the phrase which best describes it.

1. ___ sonnet   a. generally a silly poem of five lines

2. ___ soliloquy   b. a story about a real person written by another person

3. ___ fantasy   c. 14 line poem with a specific rhyme scheme

4. ___ biography   d. a story with make believe creatures

5. ___ autobiography   e. a speech in a play, in which the speaker is talking to himself

6. ___ myth   f. a story which may have a moral or teach a lesson

7. ___ limerick   g. a story about a person written by themself

8. ___ palindrome   h. a word with a double meaning, generally used in a funny way

9. ___ pun   i. a word or phrase which spells the same frontwards and back

Match the following literary terms with their description.

1. ___ setting   a. the high point of a story

2. ___ sequence   b. the order of events in a story

3. ___ plot   c. time and place in which a story is set

4. ___ climax   d. exaggeration

5. ___ hyperbole   e. a brief summary of a story

6. ___ irony   a. a comparison of two unlike things

7. ___ metaphor   b. a comparison of two unlike things using "like" or "as"

8. ___ simile   c. a phrase having a literal meaning and a figurative one

9. ___ personification   d. contrast between what is expected and what actually happens

10. ___ pun   e. attributing a non-human thing with human characteristics

11. ___ analogy   a. a poem which does not rhyme

12. ___ alliteration   b. comparison between two things to show similarity

13. ___ free verse   c. words near each other beginning with the same letter

14. ___ allusion   d. plot stage where characters and setting is introduced

15. ___ exposition   e. to refer to a person, place or event – real or fictional

16. ___ flashback   a. character pitted against another character or outside force

17. ___ foreshadow   b. conflict that occurs within a character's mind

18. ___ external conflict   c. interruption of the action to present earlier events

19. ___ internal conflict   d. problems that make it more difficult to resolve the conflict

20. ___ plot complication   e. prepares readers for something to happen later in a story

Many years had passed since the last time Marta had seen her family. They lived only one planet away, but space travel was not always reliable. She knew now, though, that she needed to go, needed to see the family, needed to speak to her mother. Her mother knew things that Marta needed to know. But she didn't have money to get the interplanetary shuttle. Her job barely gave her enough money to put food on her table and keep a roof over her head. She had looked for an extra job, but no one seemed to be hiring. So now she was trying to think of what she might own that she could sell for the money she needed.

1. This story is probably   a. a soliloquy   b. a fantasy   c. biography

2. What in the story tells you this? _____

_____

3. What is the conflict Marta faces? _____

_____

4. What has she already done to try to resolve the conflict? _____

_____

_____

5. What is she thinking about doing now to resolve her conflict? _____

_____

_____

Skills of the Week

- ✔ Ratios
- ✔ Reading Comprehension
- ✔ Percent
- ✔ Clauses
- ✔ Central theme
- ✔ Finding a discount
- ✔ Science - test a hypothesis
- ✔ Summary
- ✔ Calculating simple interest
- ✔ Sequence of events

Weekly Value Honesty

Canesha Blackman

Honesty means being fair, truthful, and trustworthy. Honesty means telling the truth no matter what. People who are honest do not lie, cheat, or steal.

Sometimes it is not easy to tell the truth, especially when you are scared and do not want to get in trouble or let others down. Try to remember that even when it is difficult telling the truth is always the best way to handle any situation and people will respect you more.

Stretching is Very Important
Get into the habit of stretching every night before you go to bed, as well as before you exercise every day.

Play 60 Every Day!
Run, jump, dance and have fun outside every day for 60 minutes!

Health and Wellness

"Why are girls my age taller than boys?" Girls get a "jump start" on puberty and grow taller. Don't worry...boys will catch up in a couple years!

WEEK 1

Check the ☑ As You Complete Your Daily Task

	Day 1	Day 2	Day 3	Day 4	Day 5
MIND	☐	☐	☐	☐	☐
BODY	☐	☐	☐	☐	☐
DAILY READING	☐ 30 minutes	☐ 30 minutes	☐ 30 minutes	☐ 30 minutes	☐ 30 minutes

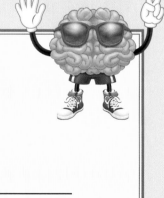

"I am honest"

_____
Print Name

Ratio

A ratio is a comparison of two quantities. It can be written more than one way, but they are read the same way. If a ratio is written 2:3, you would read it, " Two to three". Another way to write a ratio is as a fraction, which may or may not be reduced to lowest terms.

If there are 21 boys on a team, and 13 girls, the ratio of boys to girls is 21:13.

Use the chart to write some ratios.

Band Members	Boys	Girls	Total
Flutes	18	15	33
Trumpet	15	20	35
Clarinets	7	8	15
Saxophones	21	20	41
Drums	15	21	36

1. The ratio of saxophones to drums is _____

2. The ratio of flutes to clarinets is_____

3. The ratio of girls to boys in the drum section is _____

4. The ratio of girls to boys in trumpets is _____

5. The ratio of boys to girls in the saxophone section is _____

Challenge What ratio could you simplify to have a final answer of 4 : 3? _____

Science: Form a hypothesis

A hypothesis is an educated guess that can be tested. It attempts to account for the data at hand.

The first step is to collect as many observations as possible about the problem you are trying to examine. Then consider your observations and think about how they might relate to the problem. Try to imagine possible solutions to explain your observations.

Once you come up with a possible explanation, ask yourself if it could be proven wrong by an experiment. If it could be proven wrong, then you have formed a hypothesis. If there is no way to prove it wrong, go back to your data and try to come up with another hypothesis.

Assume that you have plants in the living room and in the kitchen. The plants in the kitchen, which are geraniums, seem to be healthier than those in the living room, which are pansies. The sun seems to come in the kitchen windows earlier in the day and stronger, because the windows face the south. The sun in the living room is less strong and the windows face the north.

What hypothesis can you form based on these observations?

_____

_____

_____

_____

Aerobic
Go to www.summerfitlearning.com for more Activities!

DAILY EXERCISE
Jogging for Fitness 5
"Stretch Before You Play!"

Instruction
Jog 5 minutes in place or outside

Be Healthy!
Anytime you start a new exercise routine check with a parent!

DAY 1

2

3

4

5

WEEK 1

Comprehension

From *Rikki-tikki-tavi* by Rudyard Kipling

From the thick grass at the foot of the bush came a low hiss – a horrid cold sound that made Rikki-tikki jump back two clear feet. Then inch by inch out of the grass rose up the head and spread hood of Nag, the big black cobra, and he was five feet long from tongue to tail. When he had lifted one third of himself clear of the ground, he stayed balancing to and fro exactly as a dandelion tuft balances in the wind, and he looked at Rikki-tikki with the wicked snake's eyes that never change their expression, whatever the snake may be thinking of.

"Who is Nag?" he said. "I am Nag. The great god Brahm put his mark upon all our people when the first cobra spread his hood to keep the sun of Brahm as he slept. Look, and be afraid!"

He spread out his hood more than ever, and Rikki-tikki saw the spectacle mark on the back of it that looks exactly like the eye part of a hook-and-eye fastening. He was afraid for the minute; but it is impossible for a mongoose to stay frightened for any length of time, and though Rikki-Tikki had never met a live cobra before, his mother had fed him on dead ones, and he knew that all a grown mongoose's business in life was to fight and eat snakes. Nag knew that too, and at the bottom of his cold heart he was afraid.

"Behind you! Look behind you!" sang Darzee.

Rikki-tikki knew better than to waste time in staring. He jumped up in the air as high as he could go and just under him whizzed by the head of Nagaina, Nag's wicked wife. She had crept up behind him as he was talking, to make an end of him, and he heard her savage hiss as the stroke missed. He came down almost across her back, and if he had been an old mongoose he would have known that then was the time to break her back with one bite. But he was afraid of the terrible lashing return stroke of the cobra. He bit, indeed, but did not bite long enough, and he jumped clear of the whisking tail, leaving Nagaina torn and angry.

1. What kind of animal is Rikki-tikki-tavi? _____

2. What kind of animal is Nag? _____

3. How did Rikki feel when he first met Nag? _____

4. How did Nag feel when he first met Rikki? _____

5. According to Kipling, what is a grown mongoose's business in life? _____

_____

6. Is Rikki a grown mongoose? What evidence is there in the story? _____

_____

7. Which characters are in conflict in this story? _____

Percent

A percent compares a number to 100. The % symbol means per hundred. It can be thought of as a ration of a number to 100. 50% is the ratio of 50 to 100, so a percent can be written as a fraction of 100. This should be written in lowest terms. A fraction can be written as a percent by writing an equivalent fraction with a denominator of 100, then written in percent form.

Examples $75\% = \dfrac{75}{100} = \dfrac{3}{4}$ $\dfrac{3}{5} = \dfrac{60}{100} = 60\%$

1. 30% =

2. 66% =

3. 25% =

4. 85% =

5. 48% =

6. $\dfrac{51}{100} =$

7. $\dfrac{13}{25} =$

8. $\dfrac{5}{8} =$

9. $\dfrac{7}{10} =$

10. $\dfrac{72}{72} =$

Clauses

A clause is a collection of words that has a subject that is actively doing a verb. The following are examples of clauses:

- As he was cleaning his room
- Since they were late for class
- Because she smiled at him

If the clause could stand by itself, and form a complete sentence with punctuation, we call the clause an independent clause. The following are independent clauses:

- She is going to the movie on her own
- Mary was fishing with her dad

Independent clauses could be sentences if correctly punctuated. Dependent clauses have a subject doing a verb, but they have a subordinate conjunction placed in front of the clause. That subordinate conjunction means that the clause can't stand independently by itself and become a complete sentence. Instead, the dependent clause is dependent upon another clause—it can't make a complete sentence by itself, even though it has a subject doing a verb.

Here are some examples of dependent clauses:

- Since they were late for class
- When she told him the excuse

Decide if each of the following is a Dependent (D) clause or and Independent (I) clause.

1. ___ Joaquin left the baby alone

2. ___ The boys teased Theresa

3. ___ After Martha cooked the dinner

4. ___ Because the children were on the computer

5. ___ Since they were going to the movie later

6. ___ Rosanna was tying a knot

1

DAY
2

3

4

5

WEEK 1

© Summer Fit   **21**

DAILY EXERCISE
Inchworm
"Stretch Before You Play!"

Instruction
Do 10-15 times

Be Healthy!
Help set the table for dinner today!

Central Theme

Many pieces of literature are just good stories. More often than not, however, there is a theme embedded in the story – a point that the author is trying to make. It might be about a moral issue, a human frailty, love or fate.

In the mythology, heroism is a common theme. Quite often, in myths of many civilizations, the main character of the story begins as a non-descript sort of person, with nothing much to set them apart from others. By the end of the story, this person has become a hero – often by saving others from some terrible fate or performing some difficult task. Sometimes they are blessed with uncommon strength, incredible bravery, a good deal of generosity and kindness.

One mythological hero was Hercules. He went to the Underworld and rescued others. He defeated the Hydra, a water snake with nine heads. He had to fight several supernatural creatures over the years and complete several tasks for other people. Another hero was Perseus. He decapitated the Gorgon Medusa and rescued Andromeda from a sea monster. Achilles was one of the greatest soldiers in the Trojan War. He was unbeatable until his weakness, his heel, was discovered. Atlanta was a huntress. She loved hunting and the outdoors. She frequently won hunting matches and even wrestling matches.

One heroine in Egyptian mythology is Isis. She taught the Egyptians about marriage, household management, medicine, weaving, motherhood, and the working of magical spells and charms. She was perhaps best known as the goddess of life. She represented the great parts of women: love, loyalty, protection, and motherhood. Upon hearing of Osiris's death, she instantly went into mourning and frantic searching to find him. She found and lost him again, but in the end was successful in restoring all of his body but one part.

Heroes possess many positive qualities. They are often brave. They are concerned about the less fortunate. They fight for what is right and just, even when the odds are against them. They are persistent in the pursuit of their goals.

Answer the questions below as True or False.

1. _____ Heroes are always heroes from the beginning of the story.

2. _____ One quality of heroes is bravery.

3. _____ Achilles was unbeatable until his weakness, his right hand, was injured.

4. _____ Isis was an Egyptian heroine who represented the best parts of women.

5. _____ Hercules was a hero who rescued other people.

6. _____ Perseus rescued Andromeda from a sea monster.

7. _____ A hero is usually only concerned with their own reputation.

8. _____ Heroism is a theme common in literature.

Discount is the difference between the "regular" retail price of an item and the price that a consumer actually pays for the item. To determine what the discount is multiply the regular price by the percent of the discount. Then subtract the discount from the regular price.

Example: A shirt's regular price is $25.98.

The discount is 15% off. $25.98 x 0.15 = $3. 89

The sale price is $25.98 – 3.89 = $22.09

Find the sale price for a pair of jeans: regular price $36.50; discount 20%.

Find the sale price for a hat: regular price $57.00; discount 12%.

Find the sale price for a pair of shoes: regular price $72.00; discount 25%.

Science: Design steps to test a hypothesis

Part of the scientific process is to test your hypothesis. You think that plants grow better in your kitchen, where there is a southern exposure to the sun, than in your living room, where there is a northern exposure. Read the steps below to decide which ones would be the best steps to test your hypothesis. Mark those that work with a **Y** and those that don't with an **N**.

1. _____ Have two small plants and one large one.

2. _____ Have four plants the same size and type.

3. _____ Put one plant in the living room and 2 in the closet.

4. _____ Put two plants in the kitchen and two in the living room.

5. _____ Water and care for all the plants at the same time and in the same way.

6. _____ Water the kitchen plants in the morning and the living room plants in the evening.

7. _____ Give the kitchen plants fertilizer and not the living room plants.

8. _____ Give all the plants fertilizer or none of the plants.

DAY 3

WEEK 1

1 2 4 5

Aerobic
Go to www.summerfitlearning.com for more Activities!

DAILY EXERCISE
Jump the Line
"Stretch Before You Play!"

Instruction
Perform 10 times

Be Healthy!
Stretch every night before you go to bed.

1

2

DAY 3

4

5

WEEK 1

Summary

A summary is a brief description of a story. It should tell the main characters, and the major plot events. It should not have details such as complete descriptions or dialogue. It can tell the ending, but very often does not.

To write a summary, use your own words to express briefly the main idea and relevant details of the piece you have read. Your purpose in writing the summary is to give the basic ideas of the original reading. What was it about and what did the author want to communicate?

While reading the original work, take note of what or who is the focus and ask the usual questions that reporters use: Who? What? When? Where? Why? How? Using these questions to examine what you are reading can help you to write the summary.

Identify the title and author. You may want to use this formula:

In "Title of the Piece", (name of the author) shows that (central idea of the piece).

Read the following summary, then answer the questions.

In *The Adventures of Tom Sawyer*, Mark Twain is telling a "coming of age" story. Tom is an orphaned boy who is being raised by his aunt, and he is a trial to her. He is constantly getting in trouble at school, at Sunday School, and at home. Tom is not a bad boy, but he seems to consistently make bad choices.

The story takes place in Missouri during the mid 1800s. The children play outside and make up the games that they play. Adult supervision is much looser than it is today, with children being out and away from home much of the day.

Tom is involved with lots of normal and healthy shenanigans. He is well liked by the other children and is a happy child most of the time. But in this story he deals with his first love, which causes him heartache and stress. And he witnesses a murder, and is faced with a terrible choice: let an innocent man hang or tell what he knows and face danger from the real murderer.

1. What is the name of the work being summarized? _____

_____

2. Who wrote the book? _____

3. Where does Tom get into trouble? _____

4. When does the story take place and where? _____

5. What two things look like the conflicts Tom will face in the story? _____

_____

Calculating simple interest

Simple interest is generally charged for borrowing money for short periods of time. When money is borrowed, interest is charged for the use of that money for a certain period of time. When the money is paid back, the principal (amount of money that was borrowed) and the interest is paid back. The amount to interest depends on the interest rate, the amount of money borrowed (principal) and the length of time that the money is borrowed.

The formula for finding simple interest is: Interest = Principal x Rate x Time. If $100 was borrowed for 2 years at a 10% interest rate, the interest would be $100 x 10/100 x 2 = $20. The total amount that would be due would be $100 + $20 = $120.

1. Ray borrowed $250 at 12% interest for 3 years. What amount is due in 3 years?

2. Dermot borrowed $875 at 17% interest for 2 years. What amount is due in 2 years?

3. Leonard borrowed $98 at 4.99% interest for 2 years. What amount is due in 2 years?

1 2 3 DAY 4 5

Place

A second theme of Geography is place. Place refers to what sets a structure or area apart from others – what is unique about it. For example, a home is very different from a museum. There may be elements in common – they both have furniture, people move around in them, they are lit and heated or cooled, but there are definite differences. People live in homes, but not in museums. The furniture in homes is for people to use, in museums the furniture is used as exhibits. Museums have specific hours when visitors can have access; a home is open to the people who live there at any time.

Use the chart below to find similarities and differences between a mall and a school.

	Mall	School
Layout	**Long hallways**	
Rooms		**Many rooms**
What is in rooms		**Desks**
Purpose of place		**Learning**
Who is there	**Clerks, shoppers**	

WEEK 1

DAILY EXERCISE
Grasshopper Crunch
"Stretch Before You Play!"

Instruction
Repeat 5-10 times

Be Healthy!
Talk about your day with your family.

1
2
3
DAY 4
5

WEEK 1

Sequence of Events

After losing the key to his house, Rafael decided he needed to retrace his steps of the day. He hoped that he would be able to figure out where he had lost the key.

He had begun the day by meeting his friend, Leonard, at Leonard's house. They met to work on their project for the science exposition that would happen on Tuesday. They worked in Leonard's room, but Rafael was fairly sure he didn't lose the key there. He hadn't had his hands in his pockets, so he was pretty sure he hadn't pulled the key out accidentally.

Next, he went to the arcade with Stephan. He had to get money from his wallet, but that was in the back pocket, which was not where he kept the key. He had gone to the ice cream shop, and met Sandy there. They had ice cream sodas and talked for a while, but he didn't think he had the key with him then. He had gotten change from his pocket to leave the tip, and now he didn't remember feeling the key. Right before the ice cream shop, he had stopped at the bicycle shop to see if his bike repair was finished. Maybe he had lost the key there. He did remember getting the claims check out of his pocket, and thought he had felt the key. He knew some change had fallen out, and he was pretty sure he had picked it all up, but he hadn't noticed the key at the time.

Now that he thought he knew where the key was, he went back to the bicycle shop. He asked the clerk, Sophie, who was a friend of his, if anyone had turned in a key. She laughed and said that yes, someone had given her a key shortly after he had left. She had wondered then if it was his, as he had seemed flustered when he had spilled his change. So he got the key from her and was able to head home.

Put the events of the story in the order in which they originally occurred.

_____ Went to the bike shop for the first time

_____ Went to the bike shop for the second time

_____ Met Sandy at the ice cream shop

_____ Decided to retrace his steps

_____ Went to the arcade with Stephan

_____ Met Leonard at his house

_____ Went home to stay

HONESTY - Canesha Blackman

What is honesty? It is the quality which allows you to tell the truth and do what is right, no matter how tempting it might be to do otherwise.

Imagine that you are 24, you are homeless, and you have 5 children. You are single because of a bad marriage. You have to try to scrape together enough bus fare to get to your job. Then, one day, you find a bag outside of a city building. Do you look inside? Do you try to use what you find for yourself?

Canesha Blackman didn't look inside, didn't try to find out if the bag could help her – she just took it into the city building and turned it in. The bag had $800 and belonged to a sheriff's detective of Polk County, Florida. When the money was returned to him, he went to the Salvation Army homeless shelter to thank Ms. Blackman.

Her honesty has been rewarded by an outpouring of gifts and aid from the community. But Blackman doesn't think she did anything special. What do you think?

1. Why was Canesha struggling financially? _____

2. Who do you know that demonstrates honesty? How do they do this? _____

_____

_____

3. Why might it have been difficult for Canesha to give back the money he found? _____

_____

_____

_____

4. How has Canesha been rewarded for her honesty? _____

_____

_____

_____

Color a star for each time you show Honesty through your own actions this week.

 Write a 50-75 word essay describing one of your Honesty actions this week.

Honesty – Memorize Your Value

"No legacy is so rich as honesty."

– William Shakespeare

1

2

3

4

DAY
5

WEEK 1

Core Value Booklist
Read More About Honesty

Nothing But the Truth
by Avi

Caleb's Choice
by G. Clifton Wisler

Moves Make the Man
by Bruce Brooks

The Shakespeare Stealer
by Gary L. Blackwood

Zach's Lie
by Roland Smith

.........TECH TIME!..........

How do you see honesty represented by Canesha Blackman? Use a web 2.0 presentation tool to share what you know of her in 4-6 creative slides. Think of a catchy phrase or two to put on some slides that show her honesty. Share what you have made with as many people as you can!

www.SummerFitLearning.com

Bill Gates
Tech Guru and
Philanthropist
gatesfoundation.org

Play Time!
Choose a Game or Activity to Play for 60 minutes today!

YOU CHOOSE

Write down which game or activity you played today!

Be Healthy!
Drink water instead of sugary soda drinks.

PARENT TIPS FOR WEEK 2

Skills of the Week

✔ Scale

✔ Geographic theme of Movement

✔ Sonnet

✔ Parentheses, dashes

✔ Decimals, fractions, percents

✔ Simile

✔ Punctuation for direct quotations

✔ Human Environment Interaction

✔ Soliloquy

✔ Metaphor

✔ Affixes and roots

Weekly Value Compassion

Eleanor Roosevelt

Compassion is caring about the feelings and needs of others.

Sometimes we are so focused on our own feelings that we don't care how other people feel. If we consider other's feelings before our own the world can be a much kinder place. Take time to do something nice for another person and you will feel better about yourself.

GET FIT TIME!

Stretching is Very Important

Get into the habit of stretching every night before you go to bed, as well as before you exercise every day.

Play 60 Every Day!

Run, jump, dance and have fun outside every day for 60 minutes!

Health and Wellness

What are "growing pains?" No, they're not a disease. These pains are telling you that your body is growing up! Most of the time the pains are in the legs and hurt more at bedtime. Sometimes, they may even wake you up. The good news is that they go away around 13 years old. Doing the daily stretches in this book can help them feel better!

WEEK 2

HEALTHY MIND + HEALTHY BODY

Check the ☑ As You Complete Your Daily Task

	Day 1	Day 2	Day 3	Day 4	Day 5
MIND	☐	☐	☐	☐	☐
BODY	☐	☐	☐	☐	☐
DAILY READING	☐ 30 minutes	☐ 30 minutes	☐ 30 minutes	☐ 30 minutes	☐ 30 minutes

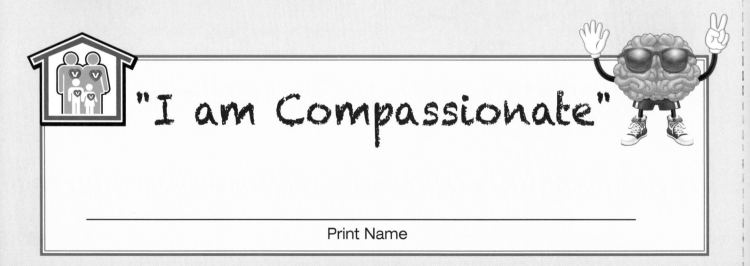

"I am Compassionate"

_____

Print Name

Scale

It is not always possible to draw on paper the actual size of real-life objects such as the real size of a car, or an airplane. We need scale drawings to represent the size.

In reality, this car may be 200 inches long. You could not fit a drawing that size on a piece of paper. So we use a scale, such as 1 inch representing 20 inches. Your drawing would be 10 inches.

The scale would be written the same as a ration, such as 1:20. The first number refers to the drawing or map, and the second number to the real life object. You would determine the real length by setting up a proportion. It would look like this: **Length of drawing = 1**

1. If the length of your drawing is 12 inches, what is the real length of the object?

_____

Movement

Movement is a third theme of Geography. This theme includes movement of people, animals, goods, and ideas.

One great example of movement is the theory of migration across the Bering Land Bridge in prehistoric times. There had been major climate changes. Glaciers were growing, water levels were dropping, and the land bridge between Asia and Alaska became usable. Animals began to cross, looking for new grazing or hunting grounds. People followed the animal herds. The migration continued for hundreds of years. The people spread over North America and south to Central and eventually South America.

Another example of movement deals with the printing press. Before the invention of the printing press, only a few people could read and write, and there was little material available to read anyway. After the press was invented, books became more accessible to people and more people began to learn to read. Ideas that began in Germany were able to be printed, and later read by people in England and Italy. So those ideas moved across the European continent.

1. There were four things listed in the text which can be "moved". What are they?

_____

_____

2. What was moved across the Bering Land Bridge? _____

_____

_____

3. What was moved due to the printing press? _____

_____

_____

Aerobic

Go to www.summerfitlearning.com for more Activities!

DAILY EXERCISE
Crooked Bunny
"Stretch Before You Play!"

Instruction
Perform 3 times in place or outside

Be Healthy!
Wash your hands before every meal.

DAY 1
2 3 4 5

WEEK 2

Sonnet

A sonnet is a particular style of poetry. The name comes from an Italian word "sonetto" which means little song. Traditionally, is has 14 lines of iambic pentameter – huh!? That just means that every line has 10 syllables and every other syllable is stressed (soft – LOUD - soft – LOUD - soft – LOUD - soft – LOUD - soft – LOUD).

There are different possible rhyme schemes. The sonnet below has this scheme: ABBA ABBA CDC DCD. (This is different from the scheme Shakespeare followed.)

William Shakespeare, who lived in England in the late 1500s and early 1600s, is considered by many to be the greatest writer in the English language. However, other people have written sonnets as well. Elizabeth Barrett Browning lived in the 1800s. She was one of the most prominent poets of her time. She married the poet Robert Browning who was also very popular at the time. The poem below is from her book, Sonnets from the Portuguese, dedicated to her husband.

Sonnet XLIII
How do I love thee? Let me count the ways.
I love thee to the depth and breadth and height
My soul can reach, when feeling out of sight
For the ends of Being and ideal Grace.
I love thee to the level of everyday's
Most quiet need, by sun and candle-light.
I love thee freely, as men strive for Right;
I love thee purely, as they turn from Praise.
I love thee with a passion put to use
In my old griefs, and with my childhood's faith.
I love thee with a love I seemed to lose
With my lost saints,--I love thee with the breath,
Smiles, tears, of all my life! –and, if God choose,
I shall but love thee better after death.

1. In addition to rhyme at the ends of the lines, Browning uses some internal rhyme (rhyming within a line). What is the internal rhyme in line 2? _____

_____

2. Anaphora is a literary technique in which a word or words at the beginning of two or more verses in a row are repeated. What phrase is repeated at the beginning of several lines in the poem?

_____

_____

3. Browning also used alliteration in the sonnet (two or more words close together with same beginning sound). Give an example from line 8. _____

_____

Converting a decimal to a fraction

Converting a decimal to a fraction is very simple. The decimal is already "read" in terms of tenths, hundredths, or thousandths. Simply make the numerator the number that is behind the decimal, and the denominator is the tenths, hundredths, or thousandths – then simplify. If there is a whole number (in the ones or tens place for instance) it remains a whole number.

Example:

$$0.32 = \frac{32}{100} = \frac{8}{25} \qquad 0.045 = \frac{45}{1000} = \frac{9}{200} \qquad 2.55 = 2\frac{55}{100} = 2\frac{11}{20}$$

Try your own:

1. $0.25 = $ _____

2. $0.038 = $ _____

3. $0.33 = $ _____

4. $4.12 = $ _____

5. $2.22 = $ _____

6. $4.75 = $ _____

7. $1.1 = $ _____

8. $2.5 = $ _____

Simile

A simile is a comparison of two things using like or as. **Example:** Charlie was like a walking calculator with his quick math skills. Similes are often used with poetry. Such as the poem *A Red, Red Rose* by Robert Burns.

> O my luve's like a red, red rose,
>   That's newly sprung in June;
> O my luve's like the melodie
>   That's sweetly played in tune.

Decide if each line below is a simile or not, if so mark it with an <u>S</u>. If not, mark it with an <u>N</u> and turn it into a simile.

1. _____ Santa's belly jiggled like a bowl of jelly when he laughed. _____

_____

2. _____ The bowl was cracked and so it leaked. _____

_____

3. _____ The dust on the piano was an inch thick. _____

_____

DAILY EXERCISE
Ninja Crawl
"Stretch Before You Play!"

Instruction
Crawl for 5 minutes

Be Healthy!
Give your parents a hug.

1

DAY 2

3

4

5

WEEK 2

Punctuation for direct quotation

Quotation marks are used to enclose a person's exact words when speaking. This is called a direct quotation. An indirect quotation also tells what a person said, but does not quote their exact words. Sometimes what a person said is written on both sides of the speaker's name: "What should we wear for the party," asked Eleanor, "if it is going to be in the park?" Notice that the punctuation for the sentence in the quotation is within the quotation marks.

In the following sentences, determine whether it is a direct or indirect quotation. Write a D if it is direct and write an I if it is indirect. If it is a direct quotation, add the quotation marks correctly.

1. ___ Kat said that she wanted ice cream.
2. ___ Bailey asked when the game would begin.
3. ___ Dad said Would you please stop annoying your sister?
4. ___ The football team shouted in unison Go, Ramblers!!
5. ___ Nathan Hale said I regret that I have but one life to give for my country.
6. ___ Bobby told her mother that she would be home after the play.
7. ___ The president said that he would do his best for the country.
8. ___ Jackson yelled at his dog for barking so loudly.

Parentheses, dashes

Rule 1: Use parentheses to enclose words or figures that clarify or are used as an aside.
Examples: I wanted to go to the movie at the mall (the new mall downtown).
Rule 2: Use full parentheses to enclose numbers or letters used for listed items.
Example: It helps your career if you (1) have the proper training, (2) are motivated, and (3) work hard.
Rule 3: The dash is used to indicate a sudden or abrupt change in thought.
Example: I will write the letter – but someone's at the door.
Rule 4: The dash may be used to enclose material which could be in parenthesis.
Example: Sometime next week – I forget when – I have an appointment.
Rule 5: The dash is used before a word that sums up a preceding list of words.
Example: English, mathematics, and science – these are important high school subjects.
If parentheses or dashes are used correctly, mark the sentence with a C – if not, mark with an X.

1. ___ Write a short essay on pets (be sure to include a brief description of our class pet).
2. ___ The contract is due within thirty (30) days.
3. ___ Marianne went to the store (to buy pens for her project).
4. ___ I would like to get some swim time in (wait, I forgot to get my suit!)
5. ___ You should read (1) a biography, (2) a mystery, and (3) a novel.
6. ___ Ricardo went to (1) the store, (2) to buy, (3) some candy.
7. ___ We can go to the movie – but I need to get money from the bank!

Convert decimal to percent

Decimals can be written as a percent very simply. The decimal 0.43 is read as 43 hundredths, meaning 43 out of 100, which can also be written 43%. 43% also means 43 out of 100, or 43 hundredths, which is 0.43

Change the following decimals to percents.

1. 0.78 _____

2. 0.50 _____

3. 0.35 _____

4. 0.72 _____

5. 1.25 _____

6. 0.63 _____

7. 3.95 _____

8. 5.10 _____

Human Environment Interaction (HEI)

A fourth theme of Geography is Human Environment Interaction. This can be positive or negative. When we do something to the environment which is helpful, that's a positive interaction. Conservation is a positive form of interaction. Conservation is involved when we work to preserve our resources. When we designate wildlife preserves or national forests, we are conserving those resources.

A negative interaction is the consistent deforestation taking place across our globe. The positive counteraction to this is reforestation. Reforestation not only renews the resources of the forests, it provides habitats for many animals. It also helps support our ozone layer and hopefully slows down the greenhouse effect which is damaging our planet.

HEI is not a new event. People have been changing the environment for as long as they have been around. One well-known example is the Olmec people of Central America. As the civilization grew, they needed to expand their farmland. However, there were dense forests nearby. The Olmec began to cut the trees from the forest. They would wait several months for the trees to dry. Then they would burn the trees, leaving the ash, which served as a fertilizer to make the new farmland more fertile. They would farm for a few years, until the land became less productive, then move on to a new forest area and begin again.

1. Why did the Olmec leave the ash on the ground? _____

_____

2. How is reforestation a positive HEI? _____

_____

3. Why is deforestation considered negative? _____

_____

4. What does conservation mean? _____

_____

Aerobic
Go to www.summerfitlearning.com for more Activities!

DAILY EXERCISE
Burpies
"Stretch Before You Play!"

Instruction
Perform 5-7 times

Be Healthy!
Playing, running and jumping make you stronger.

1

2

DAY 3

4

5

WEEK 2

Soliloquy

One way to think of a soliloquy is that it's a speech you make to yourself. An author may have a character give a soliloquy in order for the reader to understand the character's thoughts and perspective. A more formal definition is a dramatic speech that represents reflections or unspoken thoughts by the character.

Here is a modern version of Juliet's soliloquy in Romeo and Juliet. Even though Romeo hears her, it is considered a soliloquy because she doesn't know he is listening, so she is just talking to herself.

Oh, Romeo, Romeo, why do you have to be Romeo? Forget about your father and change your name. Or else, if you won't change your name, just swear you love me and I'll stop being a Capulet.

It's only your name that's my enemy. You'd still be yourself even if you stopped being a Montague. What's a Montague anyway? It isn't a hand, a foot, an arm, a face, or any other part of a man. Oh, be some other name! What does a name mean? The thing we call a rose would smell just as sweet if we called it by any other name. Romeo would be just as perfect even if he wasn't called Romeo. Romeo, lose your name. Trade in your name—which really has nothing to do with you—and take all of me in exchange.

1. What does Juliet think is the main problem between herself and Romeo, and how could it be fixed? _____

_____

_____

2. What does Juliet mean when she says Romeo's name "really has nothing to do with" him?

_____

_____

3. What does Juliet suggest could have another name and still be the same (besides Romeo)?

_____

_____

4. Juliet thinks she is talking to herself. What might she have said differently if she knew that Romeo was listening? _____

_____

_____

Convert percent to fraction

To convert a percent to a fraction, think of the percent as a fraction of 100. Sometimes a percent is more than 100. In that case, anything over 100 becomes a whole number in your mixed fraction.

Example:

$234\% = 2\dfrac{34}{100} = 2\dfrac{17}{50}$

Remember to simplify, and remember to keep the whole number with the fraction.

1. 117% _____

2. 265% _____

3. 175% _____

4. 495% _____

5. 150% _____

6. 232% _____

7. 364% _____

8. 145% _____

Metaphor

Metaphors are comparisons similar to similes. The difference is that a metaphor does not use any clue words (whereas the simile uses like or as).

Explain what is being compared in each sentence.

1. She had a heart of stone. _____

_____

2. Her soft voice was music to my ears. _____

_____

3. Life is a roller coaster which everyone has to ride. _____

_____

4. The office was his prison. _____

_____

5. Selena was a real angel. _____

_____

6. The noise of children playing was music to my ears. _____

_____

7. Many people think the business world is a real jungle. _____

_____

8. The runner was a gazelle streaking across the finish line. _____

_____

9. Education is a gateway to your destiny in life. _____

_____

DAILY EXERCISE
Dead Bug
"Stretch Before You Play!"

Instruction
Hold for 2 minutes

Be Healthy!
Always use sunscreen when you are playing outside!

Affixes and roots

Affixes are prefixes (attached to the front of a root) and suffixes (attached to the end of a root). If you know the meanings of common affixes and of common roots, you can figure out what a word means, or close to it. For example, dis- means not, so disinterested means not interested.

Here are some common prefixes and suffixes. Use them to try to figure out the meanings of the words listed below.

Prefix	Root	Suffix
Pre – before	Script – something written	Ade – act, product, sweet drink
Post – after	Informed – told about	Graphy – written about
Mis – bad, badly, wrong	Meditated – thought about	Ology – study of
Auto - self	Bio - life	

1. blockade _____

2. postscript _____

3. misinformed _____

4. premeditated _____

5. biology _____

6. autobiography _____

7. biography _____

1 2 3 DAY 4 5

WEEK 2

COMPASSION - Eleanor Roosevelt

Eleanor Roosevelt was shy as a child, which would surprise those who knew her in her later years. As the wife of President Franklin D. Roosevelt, she held press conferences and had her own newspaper column. She demonstrated compassion for others by speaking out on a variety of issues: the poor, women's rights, children's causes, racial equality, and human rights.

She shocked many people when she championed the Tuskegee Airmen. Many people were not certain that these African American pilots could be as skilled as other pilots. Eleanor visited Tuskegee, Alabama, to demonstrate her support of the program training these men. She even had one of the pilots fly her around the area to the frustration of the secret service agents assigned to her.

After her husband's death, she was a delegate to the United Nations. She was the chairperson of the UN Human Rights Commission and helped write the Universal Declaration of Human Rights. She also served as the chairperson on the Commission on the Status of Women. Eleanor used the power of her name and her position to work for those in need.

1. What are two issues Eleanor spoke out about? _____

_____

2. What is a definition of the word delegate? _____

_____

3. After reading Eleanor's story, how would you explain the value of compassion? Give an example of someone you know who demonstrates compassion.

_____

_____

_____

_____

_____

Color a star for each time you show Compassion through your own actions this week.

 Write a 50-75 word essay describing one of your Compassion actions this week.

Compassion – Memorize Your Value

"We think too much and feel too little. More than machinery, we need humanity. More than cleverness, we need kindness and gentleness."

– Charlie Chaplin (1889-1977); Comic Actor, Filmmaker, Writer

Core Value Booklist
Read More About Compassion

A Long Walk to Water
by Linda Sue Park

The Sin Eater
by Gary D Schmidt

Annie's Monster
by Barbara Corcoran

The Best Bad Thing
by Yoshiko Uchida

Madeline and the Great (Old) Escape Artist
by R. C. Jones

..........TECH TIME!..........

As you have learned, Eleanor Roosevelt was an amazing person. Go online to find a web 2.0 tool that helps you to create a digital story book. Make a short story about her. Share it with someone younger than you so they can learn about her compassion too. Let your parents and friends see what you created!

www.SummerFitLearning.com

Bill Gates
Tech Guru and Philanthropist
gatesfoundation.org

1
2
3
4

DAY 5

WEEK 2

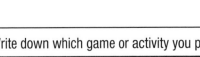

Play Time!

Choose a Game or Activity to Play for 60 minutes today!

YOU CHOOSE

Write down which game or activity you played today!

 Be Healthy!
Take breaks from the sun by moving in the shade

Skills of the Week

- ✔ Positive and negative numbers, addition, subtraction,
- ✔ Multiplication and division
- ✔ Comprehension
- ✔ Who and whom
- ✔ Regions of the United States
- ✔ Homograph
- ✔ Ecosystem
- ✔ Synonyms
- ✔ Migration and push/pull factors
- ✔ Internal conflict
- ✔ Antonyms
- ✔ Adverbs and adjectives

Weekly Value Trustworthiness

Dana Reeve

Trustworthiness is being worthy of trust. It means people can count on you.

You are honest and you keep your word. Sometimes it is easy to forget what we tell people because we try to do too much or we are constantly moving around. Try to slow down and follow through on what you say before moving onto something else.

Stretching is Very Important
Get into the habit of stretching every night before you go to bed, as well as before you exercise every day.

Play 60 Every Day!

Run, jump, dance and have fun outside every day for 60 minutes!

Health and Wellness

Get enough sleep. It helps your brain work better! You should average between 8-9 hours of sleep each day!

Check the ✓ As You Complete Your Daily Task

	Day 1	Day 2	Day 3	Day 4	Day 5
MIND	☐	☐	☐	☐	☐
BODY	☐	☐	☐	☐	☐
DAILY READING	☐	☐	☐	☐	☐
	30 minutes	30 minutes	30 minutes	30 minutes	30 minutes

"I am trustworthy"

_____
Print Name

Adding positive and negative numbers

The sum of two positive integers is a positive integer. The sum of two negative integers is a negative integer. To find the sum of a positive integer and a negative integer, you subtract the smaller absolute number from the larger one, then assign the sign of the larger one.

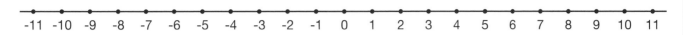

-11 -10 -9 -8 -7 -6 -5 -4 -3 -2 -1 0 1 2 3 4 5 6 7 8 9 10 11

Example: 3 + (-5)   Think (5 – 3 = 2). 5 is larger than 3 and it's sign is negative. So the answer is -2. You can also use the number line. Begin at 3 and count 5 in the negative direction. You end up at -2.

DAY 1 2 3 4 5

1. -3 + (-5) = _____

2. 9 + (-3) = _____

3. 8 + (-2) = _____

4. -7 + (-9) = _____

5. 10 + (-3) = _____

6. 6 + (-9) = _____

7. -3 + 5 = _____

8. -4 + (-5) = _____

9. 18 + (-7) = _____

10. -6 + 12 = _____

Who, whom

The correct usage of the words who and whom confuses a lot of people. Who is used as the subject of a sentence, phrase or clause. Whom is used as an object of a verb or preposition. A quick an easy hint is to substitute a pronoun for the word. If you can substitute he or she, or answer a question with he or she, then the correct word to use is who. If you can substituted him or her, or answer a question with him or her, the correct word would be whom.

In each sentence below, decide whether to use who or whom.

1. Did you give the paper to _____ it needed to go?

2. I'm not sure _____ gave the commencement speech.

3. _____ did you say wants to see me?

4. I don't know _____ was with Keyawno.

5. We like Georgette, our classmate, _____ the teacher praises.

6. Tanya knows _____ that man is.

7. _____ was Lucille writing to yesterday?

8. Donavon gave candy to all the kids _____ wanted some.

9. I know all the kids _____ go downtown on the bus.

10. Do you know to _____ the picture money goes?

WEEK 3

DAILY EXERCISE
Side Shuffles
"Stretch Before You Play!"

Instruction
10 Shuffles to the
Right and Left.
Repeat 2 x's

Be Healthy!
Exercise is
good for health,
but it also puts
you in a good
mood

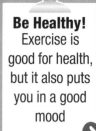

DAY 1

Reading comprehension

From *The Call of the Wild* by Jack London

Buck did not read the newspapers, or he would have known that trouble was brewing, not alone for himself, but for every tide-water dog, strong of muscle and with warm, long hair, from Puget Sound to San Diego. Because men, groping in the Arctic darkness, had found a yellow metal, and because steamship and transportation companies were booming the find, thousands of men were rushing into the Northland. These men wanted dogs, and the dogs they wanted were heavy dogs, with strong muscles by which to toil, and furry coats to protect them from the frost.

Buck was neither house-dog nor kennel-dog. The whole realm was his. He plunged into the swimming tank or went hunting with the Judge's sons; he escorted Mollie and Alice, the Judge's daughters, on long twilight or early morning rambles; on wintry nights he lay at the Judge's feet before the roaring library fire; he carried the Judge's grandsons on his back, or rolled them in the grass, and guarded their footsteps through wild adventures down to the fountain in the stable yard, and even beyond, where the paddocks were, and the berry patches. Among the terriers he stalked imperiously, and Toots and Ysabel he utterly ignored, for he was king, - king over all creeping, crawling, flying things of Judge Miller's place, humans included.

And this was the manner of the dog Buck was in the fall of 1897, when the Klondike strike dragged men from all the world into the frozen North. Buck did not read the newspapers, and he did not know that Manuel, one of the gardener's helpers, was an undesirable acquaintance. Manuel had one besetting sin, he loved to play Chinese lottery. Also, in his gambling, he had one besetting weakness - faith in a system; and this made his damnation certain. For to play a system requires money, while the wages of a gardener's helper do not lap over the needs of a wife and numerous progeny.

1. What was the yellow metal which drew men to the Northland? _____

2. Why were dogs like Buck wanted by the men going to the Arctic? _____
_____

3. What does "imperiously" mean? _____
_____

4. What was Manuel's weakness? _____
_____

5. For what, other than gambling, did Manuel need money? _____
_____

6. Predict what will happen to Buck. _____
_____

WEEK 3

Subtracting positive and negative numbers

To subtract an integer, add it's opposite.

Examples: $3 - 9 = 3 + (-9) = -6$ $-9 - 4 = -9 + (-4) = -13$ $-6 - (-5) = -6 + 5 = -1$

1. $2 - 6 =$ _____

2. $16 - 15 =$ _____

3. $-9 - (-11) =$ _____

4. $-4 - 9 =$ _____

5. $12 - (-5) =$ _____

6. $-3 - (-6) =$ _____

7. $-14 - 4 =$ _____

8. $14 - 4 =$ _____

9. $14 - (-4) =$ _____

10. $-14 - (-4) =$ _____

Regions of the United States

Region is one of the themes of geography. A region is an area that has something in common. That something could be language, land formations, shared history or culture.

The United States is divided into many types of regions. One type of division is location. The regions of this type would be the Northeast, the Southeast, the Middlewest, the Southwest, and the West.

Many of the states in the Northeast were original colonies which became the first sates. The climate consists of four distinct seasons. There are many large cities with large populations. A lot of cities are involved in shipping, trade and manufacturing.

In the Southeast are some of the other original colonies. This is a largely agricultural area, though there is shipping and manufacturing as well.

The Middlewest is the area of the Great Plains. Lots of farmland is found here, with some large cities here and there. Most of the larger cities are located along riverways.

The Southwest is small in the number of states, but large in land area. The land is largely desert and the area is strongly influenced by Native American and Hispanic cultures.

The West covers land along the Rocky Mountains and west. There is a great variety of land forms and general geography here. This region also includes Hawaii and Alaska.

1. In which region do you live? _____

2. What would you say are two characteristics of the region in which you live?

_____   _____

DAILY EXERCISE
Reach and Rotate
"Stretch Before You Play!"

Instruction
5 times

Be Healthy!
Eat breakfast
with your
family.

1

DAY 2

3

4

5

WEEK 3

Homograph

Homographs are words that are spelled the same but have different meanings.
Choose the best definition for the use of the underlined word in each sentence.

1. _____ The scratch on his arm was so minute I could barely see it.
   a. very small   **b.** a measure of time
2. _____ It was a matter of seconds before she returned with the tray of food.
   a. a helping of food after the first helping   **b.** a measure of time
3. _____ He was able to put all of his supplies into a compact package.
   a. very small   **b.** a small container of makeup
4. _____ They cleaned all of the buildings in the compound.
   a. to mix or combine   **b.** enclosed area with building or group of buildings inside
5. _____ The excess refuse was piled around the already full garbage cans.
   a. decline or reject   **b.** waste or garbage
6. _____ They used the proceeds of the sale to purchase new playground equipment.
   a. profit from a sale or venture   **b.** to move forward
7. _____ His jaw was number after the second shot from the dentist.
   a. numerical value   **b.** no feeling due to medication
8. _____ He tried to project his voice so as to be heard over the crowd.
   a. a task   **b.** to speak loudly

Adverbs and Adjectives

Adverbs and adjectives make our writing more interesting and help fill out the ideas. The difference is that adverbs modify verbs, adjectives or other adverbs, while adjectives modify nouns. Adverbs often tell when, where, why, or under what conditions something happens or happened. Adverbs frequently end in –ly, though there can be words such as lovely that are adjectives.

Determine whether the underlined word in each sentence is an adverb or an adjective.

1. _____ The test questions were <u>easy</u>.
2. _____ The students answered the questions <u>easily</u>.
3. _____ Sean has a <u>delightful</u> singing voice.
4. _____ He sings that song <u>beautifully</u>.
5. _____ My parents agreed with me <u>completely</u>.
6. _____ The chocolate dessert made the dinner <u>complete</u>.
7. _____ Armand speaks very <u>quietly</u>.
8. _____ The redwood tree was <u>extremely</u> tall.
9. _____ A cheetah runs <u>incredibly</u> quickly.
10. _____ Alison lives in a <u>friendly</u> neighborhood.

Solve problems with positive and negative numbers

1. Mt. Everest, the highest elevation in Asia, is 29,028 feet above sea level. The Dead Sea, the lowest elevation, is 1,312 feet below sea level. How far is it from the top of Mt. Everest to the Dead Sea? _____

2. The temperature started at -3 degrees this morning, and dropped another 6. What is the temperature now? _____

3. A submarine was submerged 700 feet below sea level. If it ascends 350 feet, what is its new position? _____

4. The mailman delivered 3 checks for $6 each and 2 bills for $7 each. If you had a starting balance of $25, what is the ending balance? _____

Ecosystem

Plants and animals depend on each other to survive. This connection of living things to each other is called biodiversity. An ecosystem, short for 'ecological system', includes all the living organisms existing together in a particular area. These plants and animals within an area interact with each other and with the non-living elements of the area, such as climate, water, soil and so on.

An ecosystem can be very small, such as your back yard or a puddle, or it can be huge, such as an ocean. The balance of an ecosystem is delicate. Something like the introduction of a new element can damage it. If a new animal is introduced into an ecosystem, it is in competition with the indigenous animals for food and habitat.

Humans have done quite a bit of damage to ecosystems in our world. We are responsible for oil and other wastes in our water sources. We cut down trees, slowly decreasing our forests and the ecosystems living in them. We burn garbage and pollute the air, causing problems for all creatures that breathe that air, including humans.

1. In an ecosystem, animals and plants _____ upon each other.

2. How is your backyard an example of an ecosystem? _____

_____

_____

3. What is something you can do to help improve an ecosystem in which you are involved?

_____

_____

DAILY EXERCISE
Single Leg Pop-Hops
"Stretch Before You Play!"

Instruction
Jump on each leg 10-15 times down and back

Be Healthy!
Make a healthy sandwich for lunch today with whole grain bread.

Synonyms

A synonym is a word that means the same or about the same thing as another word. Use of synonyms can help your writing become more interesting as it clarifies meaning and helps you to not be repetitive. In each set of words, circle the one which is not a synonym of the others.

1. scramble	free-for-all	order	muddle
2. keep	mislay	lose	misplace
3. decent	honorable	corrupt	moral
4. cheerful	happy	overjoyed	moody
5. grotesque	beautiful	comely	handsome
6. homely	plain	repulsive	enticing
7. obliged	grateful	critical	satisfied
8. trek	walk	tour	retire
9. gnash	stir	grind	chew
10. compliment	complaint	grievance	grumble
11. salutation	greeting	farewell	hello
12. abrupt	brusque	gradual	blunt

Antonym

An antonym is a word that is the opposite meaning of another word – such as black and white. In each set of words, circle the one that is the antonym of the others.

1. peaceful	calm	pacific	stormy
2. whole	fraction	proportion	percent
3. normal	stable	ridiculous	reasonable
4. ravenous	greedy	starved	satisfied
5. canopied	covered	open	shaded
6. wintery	balmy	tropical	temperate
7. keep	sacrifice	offer	surrender
8. labor	relax	chore	toil
9. rival	adversary	opponent	partner
10. nervous	anxious	worried	calm
11. gallant	cowardly	fearless	noble
12. faint	mild	slight	strong
13. nimble	clumsy	awkward	slow
14. optimist	hoper	pessimist	idealist

The product of two positive or two negative integers is always positive. The product of a positive integer and a negative integer is always negative. Remember that and zero is always zero.

1. -3 x (-4) = _____

2. -8 x 5 = _____

3. 5 x (-7) = _____

4. -7 x (-3) = _____

5. -8 X 0 = _____

6. -2 x 8 = _____

7. 5 x 6 = _____

8. 4 x (-9) = _____

9. -7 x (-4) = _____

10. 7 x (-4) = _____

DAY 4

1

2

3

5

WEEK 3

Push/Pull Factors of Migration

There are many reasons people decide to move from one place to another. These reasons would fall under the categories of "Push or Pull."

Push factors are those which push people out of a place. One example is famine. When people have little or no food, they would move to find a place with sufficient food. Another example is war. People leave a place to avoid war or to escape the after effects of war.

Pull factors are those which pull people to a new place. Perhaps family members have told how great a place is and so people leave to join their family. In the case of a pull factor, there may be nothing negative in the place being left; it's just that the place being moved to has something more desirable.

Label each of the following as a push factor or a pull factor.

1. _____ New, high paying jobs are being advertised.

2. _____ There are rumors of great living conditions which are very affordable

3. _____ A man has lost his job and there are no other jobs in his town

4. _____ The coal has run out in the mines and there is no work for the miners

5. _____ A group of people have been harassed because of their religious beliefs

6. _____ There is an opportunity to go to a university and get a good education

Strength Go to www.summerfitlearning.com for more Activities!

DAILY EXERCISE	Instruction	
Grasshopper Crunch	**Complete 10 on one**	**Be Healthy!**
"Stretch Before You Play!"	**side, 10 on the other**	Take breaks from the sun by moving in the shade.

1

2

3

DAY 4

5

WEEK 3

Internal Conflict

In literature, internal conflict is the struggle occurring within a character's mind. As opposed to external conflict, in which a character is dealing with some force outside of him or herself, the dilemma posed by an internal conflict is usually some ethical or emotional question.

In *Touching Spirit Bear* by Ben Mikaelsen, Cole Matthews has both external and internal conflicts. His internal conflicts mainly deal with his dissatisfaction with his life and his tendency to blame his unhappiness on other people. He is angry with his parents because his father was abusive and his mother was too afraid to stop his father. That is an external conflict. His reaction to this situation is to pick on others and get in trouble. He doesn't seem able to make good choices about his behavior. He battles within himself about how to behave and how to react to and treat other people.

In each scenario below, identify the internal conflict faced by the character.

1. Jared is late for school because he overslept. When he gets to the school office, he debates whether to accept the responsibility for his tardy, or say he got sick and had to stop at the restroom. The conflict is…

_____

2. There is a big test in math tomorrow, but there is a great show on TV that Alexis wants to see. The conflict is…

_____

3. Hank really wants the iPod in the display case. The clerk has left the case open and gone away to help someone else. The conflict is…

_____

4. Max's best friend is Robert. James has a great new video game, but he doesn't like Robert. Robert and James have both asked Max to come over after school. The conflict is…

_____

5. Several of Jan's friends are going to Sandra's party. Jan knows that her parents worry when she is out late, since her sister was in an accident. The conflict is…

_____

6. Terry knows that Sean stole a donut from the store. If Sean's dad finds out, Sean will be grounded and he is Terry's ride to the game on Friday night. The conflict is…

_____

TRUSTWORTHINESS - Dana Reeve

Who would you trust with your health, your well-being, your life? Christopher Reeve trusted his wife, Dana.

Reeve had been a popular movie star, but an accidental fall while riding a horse left him paralyzed from the neck down. He could not dress himself, feed himself or move on his own. He was totally dependent on others to do the normal things that we take for granted.

Dana Reeve not only was there to help with all his needs, she never gave up on him. At one point, Christopher thought maybe they should give up, just let himself die, but Dana said, "But you're still you and I love you." That gave him the will to keep pushing.

Together the Reeves began the Christopher and Dana Reeve Foundation to help improve the daily lives of people living with paralysis. Dana was the person Christopher and their family could trust to hold them all together.

DAY 5

1. How did Reeve sustain his injury? _____

_____

2. Define the word paralyzed: _____

_____

3. What is the purpose of the Christopher and Dana Reeve Foundation? _____

_____

4. Write about a person you think is trustworthy: _____

_____

_____

_____

_____

_____

Color a star for each time you show
Trustworthiness through your own actions this week.

 Write a 50-75 word essay describing one of your Trustworthiness actions this week.

Trustworthiness – Memorize Your Value

"Relationships of trust depend on our willingness to look not only to our own interests, but also the interests of others."

– Peter Farquharson

Core Value Booklist
Read More About Trustworthiness

Wish You Well
by David Baldacci

The Cay
by Theodore Taylor

To Kill A Mockingbird
by Harper Lee

A Place Called Ugly
by Avi

The Trial of Anna Cottman
by Vivien Alcock

.........TECH TIME!..........

Making a cloud of words can be fun, especially if you also make those clouds into certain shapes. Find a web 2.0 tool that helps you create shapes of word clouds. Choose ten words that go with trustworthiness and the story of Dana Reeves. Make a shaped word cloud and share it with your parents.

www.SummerFitLearning.com

Bill Gates
Tech Guru and
Philanthropist
gatesfoundation.org

1
2
3
4

DAY 5

WEEK 3

Play Time!

Choose a Game or Activity to Play for 60 minutes today!

YOU CHOOSE

_____
Write down which game or activity you played today!

Be Healthy!
Good sources of protein are meat, fish and eggs.

WEEK 4

Skills of the Week

- ✔ Area and circumference
- ✔ Limerick
- ✔ Common spelling errors
- ✔ Layers of the earth
- ✔ Rhyme scheme
- ✔ Direct and indirect quotations
- ✔ Natural resources
- ✔ Fantasy
- ✔ Direct and indirect objects
- ✔ Properties of operations
- ✔ Homophones

Weekly Value Self-Discipline

Kristi Yamaguchi

Self-discipline means self-control. It is working hard and getting yourself to do what is important.

It is easy to lose interest in what you are doing, especially if it does not come fast and easy. Focus your attention on what you are trying to accomplish and try to block out other things until you reach your goal.

Stretching is Very Important
Get into the habit of stretching every night before you go to bed, as well as before you exercise every day.

Play 60 Every Day!

Run, jump, dance and have fun outside every day for 60 minutes!

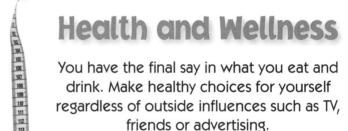

Health and Wellness

You have the final say in what you eat and drink. Make healthy choices for yourself regardless of outside influences such as TV, friends or advertising.

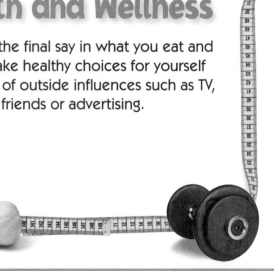

WEEK 4

Check the ☑ As You Complete Your Daily Task

	Day 1	Day 2	Day 3	Day 4	Day 5
MIND	☐	☐	☐	☐	☐
BODY	☐	☐	☐	☐	☐
DAILY READING	☐ 30 minutes	☐ 30 minutes	☐ 30 minutes	☐ 30 minutes	☐ 30 minutes

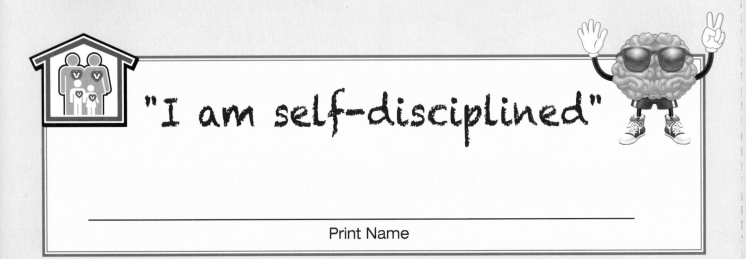

"I am self-disciplined"

_____

Print Name

Finding the area and circumference of a circle

The circumference of a circle is the actual length around the circle. Pi (π) is the number needed to compute the circumference of the circle. π is equal to 3.14.

The circumference is 3.14 (π) times the Diameter. Thus the formula is $2\pi r$ or πd.

The area is equal to 3.14 (π) times the radius (r) to the power of 2. The formula looks like

$A = \pi r2$.

Use the formula to figure out the area and circumference.

Area = _____

Circumference = _____

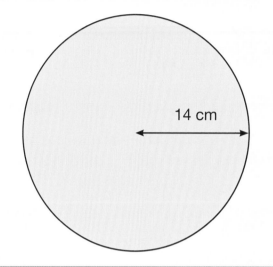

14 cm

DAY
1

2

3

4

5

WEEK 4

Spelling – common mistakes

Some words just seem to confuse people! Let's look at a few.

A lot – it's two words, not one. **Weird** (not **wierd**) – remember "we ir (are) different." **It's**, **they're** and **you're** are all contractions – respectively for it is, they are and you are. **Its**, **their**, and **your** are possessive – something belongs to it, they and you. **Affect** is a verb that you can exchange with another verb. **Effect** is a noun. **If** you can substitute a verb, effect is not the right choice. **Weather** relates to wet, dry, sunshine, wind, etc. **Whether** usually involves a choice. **Then** is in the past, than compares two things. **Past** is in the past (that's handy) and **passed** means to go by something.

See if you can use these words correctly in the sentences below. Circle the correct words to use in each sentence.

1. The cold (weather , whether) did not (affect , effect) Ethan's cold.

2. These are (you're , your) shoes, I'm sure, because they are a little (weird , weird).

3. We will buy (alot , a lot) of cookies for (they're , their) party.

4. If you (past , passed) the gas station, (then , than) we've gone too far.

5. Yesterday is in the (past , passed) so it has no (affect , effect) on my choice today.

6. I can't tell (weather , whether) he liked the book (alot , a lot) or a little.

7. Did you help the dog find (it's , its) bone, since (you're , your) here with it?

8. Will the (weather , whether) have an (affect , effect) on theparty location?

9. Would you like a toy bear rather (then , than) a toy octopus?

10. This is (they're , their) time to shine.

Aerobic

Go to www.summerfitlearning.com for more Activities!

DAILY EXERCISE
Ladders
"Stretch Before You Play!"

Instruction
**Run your course
3 times**

Be Healthy!
Choose low-fat or non-fat foods whenever you can.

DAY 1

2

3

4

5

WEEK 4

Limerick

A limerick is a humorous poem with five lines. There is a distinctive rhyme scheme: AABBA. To learn to recognize the rhythm, read the following limerick by Edward Lear.

> There was an Old Person whose habits,
> Induced him to feed upon rabbits;
> When he'd eaten eighteen,
> He turned perfectly green,
> Upon which he relinquished those habits.

The first, second, and fifth lines all have this rhythm pattern: da DUM da da DUM da da DUM (notice there are 3 DUMS or beats). Say, "There once was a fellow named Tim" out loud. Now say, "da DUM da da DUM da da DUM" out loud. Notice that both have the same rhythm. The third and fourth lines have a different rhythm pattern: da DUM da da DUM (notice there are 2 DUMS or beats). Say, "He fell off the dock" out loud. Now say "da DUM da da DUM" out loud. Notice that both have the same rhythm.

Here are a couple more limericks to enjoy.

> There was on Old Man of the Isles,
> Whose face was pervaded with smiles;
> He sung high dum diddle,
> And played on the fiddle,
> That amiable Man of the Isles.

> There was an Old Person of Dover,
> Who rushed through a field of blue Clover;
> But some very large bees,
> Stung his nose and his knees,
> So he very soon went back to Dover.

Try to write your own limerick. It helps to start with a simple name, such as, There was a young Lady names Susan, etc.

_____

_____

_____

_____

_____

Finding the area of a cube

The surface area of a cube is the area of the six squares that cover it. The area of one of them is a x a, or a^2. Since these are all the same, you can multiply one of them by six, so the surface area of a cube is 6 times one of the sides squared. Be sure to label your answer in cubic centimeters (cu. cm.)

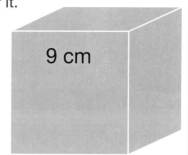

9 cm

Area = _____

Rhyme Scheme

Poets use many literary devices to make their point. One important element of many poems is rhyme. It is interesting to take note of the rhyme scheme of a poem. If you label the first line in a stanza as "a," then every line that rhymes with that line is also "a." The next ending is "b" and any line that rhymes with that line is also "b." Therefore in the poem by Ogden Nash, the rhyme scheme is AABB. In both stanzas the first two lines rhyme with each other and the second two lines rhyme with each other. This scheme is used very frequently.

***The Dog* by Ogden Nash**

The truth I do not stretch or shove
When I state the dog is full of love.
I've also proved, by actual test,
A wet dog is the lovingest.

Sometimes the rhyme scheme is irregular, as it is in *I'm Nobody* by Emily Dickinson. In this poem the rhyme scheme is AABC DEFE.

I'm Nobody

I'm nobody! Who are you?
Are you nobody, too?
Then there's a pair of us - - don't tell!
They'd banish us, you know.

How dreary to be somebody!
How public like a frog
To tell your name the livelong day
To an admiring bog.

Determine the rhyme scheme for this excerpt of a poem by Lewis Carroll.

The Walrus and the Carpenter

The sun was shining on the sea,
Shining with all his might:
He did his very best to make
The billows smooth and bright –
And this was odd, because it was
The middle of the night.

The rhyme scheme is _____

Strength

Go to www.summerfitlearning.com for more Activities!

DAILY EXERCISE
Leg Lifts
"Stretch Before You Play!"

Instruction
Repeat 5 times

Be Healthy!
Yoga is a great way to stretch, and help you focus.

Direct and Indirect Quotations

When the exact words that someone says are included in the sentence, it is a direct quotation. The author is quoting exactly what the person said. When what the person said is paraphrased, it is an indirect quotation. Notice the difference in the examples.

Direct quotation: William said, "I am too tired to stay up for the movie."
Indirect quotation: William said he was too tired to stay up for the movie.

Notice that with an indirect quotation, quotation marks are not used.

In the sentences below, determine whether each is a direct (D) or an indirect (I) quotation. If it is a direct quotation, add the quotation marks and other punctuation where necessary.

1. _____ My sister said she needed sleep.
2. _____ Anastasia is late for supper again said Fredrick.
3. _____ Alfredo came to the dance and said he was ready to show us how it's done.
4. _____ The boys said Suzanne is the best babysitter we've had.
5. _____ We can listen to the new CD in the car said Cheryl.
6. _____ All the children laughed when Mrs. Brand said she was 21.
7. _____ Bart asked Terry for some extra help with his math.
8. _____ Candi and Bette said they were ready for ice cream.
9. _____ Leigh wanted to go to the museum and he said so loudly.
10. _____ Agnes smiled and said I know the correct answer.

Layers of earth

The first layer of the earth is the crust. It consists of about 10 miles of rock and loose materials. Underneath the continents, the crust is almost three times as thick as it is under the oceans.

The next layer is the mantle. The mantle extends about 1,800 miles. It is made of a thick, solid, rocky substance. This layer makes up about 85% of the total weight and mass of the earth.

Next we come to the earth's outer core. This is as deep as 3000 miles beneath the surface. Scientists believe this is made up of super-heated liquid molten lava. They believe this is mostly made of iron and nickel.

The final layer is the inner core. It extends another 900 miles into the center of the earth. Scientists believe this is made up of a solid ball of mostly iron and nickel.

1. What two elements do scientists think are found in both the inner and outer core?

_____

2. Where is the crust thicker? _____

3. Which layer is the thinnest? _____

The basic formula for finding the area of a triangle is half of the base times the height, or the base times the height divided by two.

b = 11 cm

h = 3 cm

A = _____

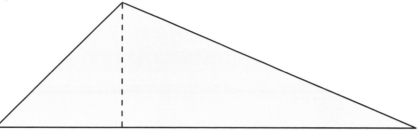

Fantasy

Writers of fantasy often create worlds and characters that can exist only in the imagination. They may be totally unreal, like the worlds in *Alice in Wonderland* and *The Hobbit*. Talking rabbits, orcs, and hobbits themselves are not found in the real world.

Other fantasy writers create realistic settings and characters, but put them in impossible situations or create impossible events. Edgar Rice Burroughs created several stories with realistic characters (and some fantastic characters) that take place on Mars. All fantasy includes at least one fantastic or unreal element.

Consider this excerpt from *Alice in Wonderland* by Lewis Carroll.

Alice was beginning to get very tired of sitting by her sister on the bank, and of having nothing to do: once or twice she had peeped into the book her sister was reading, but it had no pictures or conversations in it, `and what is the use of a book,' thought Alice `without pictures or conversation?'

So she was considering in her own mind (as well as she could, for the hot day made her feel very sleepy and stupid), whether the pleasure of making a daisy-chain would be worth the trouble of getting up and picking the daisies, when suddenly a White Rabbit with pink eyes ran close by her.

There was nothing so very remarkable in that; nor did Alice think it so very much out of the way to hear the Rabbit say to itself, `Oh dear! Oh dear! I shall be late!' (when she thought it over afterwards, it occurred to her that she ought to have wondered at this, but at the time it all seemed quite natural); but when the Rabbit actually took a watch out of its waistcoat-pocket, and looked at it, and then hurried on, Alice started to her feet, for it flashed across her mind that she had never before seen a rabbit with either a waistcoat-pocket, or a watch to take out of it, and burning with curiosity, she ran across the field after it, and fortunately was just in time to see it pop down a large rabbit-hole under the hedge.

---

1. In the first paragraph, what seems to be ordinary and realistic? _____

_____

2. What are two things about the rabbit which are not realistic? _____

_____

3. What made Alice decide to follow the rabbit? _____

_____

Aerobic

DAILY EXERCISE
Let's Roll
"Stretch Before You Play!"

Instruction
Ride for 20 Minutes

Be Healthy!
A calorie is a unit of energy.

Natural Resources

This is a list of the major resources found in several Central American countries. Look at the list carefully, then answer the questions.

Belize – arable land potential, timber, fish, hydropower

Costa Rica – hydropower

El Salvador – hydropower, geothermal power, petroleum, arable land

Guatemala – petroleum, nickel, rare woods, fish, chicle, hydropower

Honduras – timber, gold, silver, copper, lead, zinc, iron ore, antimony, coal, fish, hydropower

Mexico – petroleum, silver, copper, gold, lead, zinc, natural gas, timber

Nicaragua – gold, silver, copper, tungsten, lead, zinc, timber, fish

Panama – copper, mahogany forests, shrimp, hydropower

1. What resource is found in the most countries? _____

2. Which country has the largest variety of resources? _____

3. Which country would you infer, based on this data, has the highest Gross Domestic

   Product (GDP)? _____

4. _____

Of these eight countries, they rank as follows in GDP: Panama, Costa Rica, Mexico, Belize, El Salvador, Guatemala, Honduras, Nicaragua. **With this new information, what does this suggest about using resource information as a measurement of a country's wealth?**

_____

_____

_____

_____

WEEK 4

1 2 **DAY 3** 4 5

Properties of operations

Use properties of operations to generate equivalent statements. You can apply the associative, commutative and distributive properties and order of operations to generate equivalent expressions and to solve problems involving positive rational numbers.

Example: $\dfrac{32}{15} \times \dfrac{5}{6} = \dfrac{2 \times 16 \times 5}{3 \times 5 \times 3 \times 2} = \dfrac{16}{9} \times \dfrac{2}{2} \times \dfrac{5}{5} = \dfrac{16}{9}$

$9 \times 52 = 9 \times (50 + 2) = (9 \times 50) + (9 \times 2) = 450 + 18 = 468$

1. $8 \times 76 =$

2. $\dfrac{14}{21} \times \dfrac{36}{18} =$

Direct Object

Every sentence needs a noun and a verb. "Sarah sings." is a complete sentence. If we add the word "ballads" to the sentence, the sentence now has a direct object. In the sentence "Sarah sings ballads," the direct object is "ballads." A direct object is a noun or a pronoun that the verb in the sentence does something to. The direct object of the verb "sings" is "ballads." It's the object of the verb. Note that if we had added the word "beautifully," beautifully is not an object. It tells how Sarah sings, and is an adverb. If you can answer the question what or who after the verb, that word is the direct object. If the word tells how, when, or why, then it is not an object.

Circle the direct objects in the sentences below.

1. Matthew set the clock so that the time was correct .
2. Madeleine ordered some magazines for her mother.
3. Cassandra pushed the chair under the table.
4. Though he was already late, Jason bought coffee on his way to the office.
5. Ramon plucked the guitar strings slowly and clearly.
6. The cat meowed loudly, then slowly ate its food.
7. Jillian sat in her seat on the bus and read her book.
8. The waiter was very careful as he took our order.
9. The ball sailed over the fence and hit the car's windshield.
10. Patrick placed the flowers in the vase carefully.

DAILY EXERCISE	Instruction
Knee lifts	**Repeat 5 times**
"Stretch Before You Play!"	**with each leg**

Be Healthy!
Remember to say "thank you" to your friends and family.

Spelling - Homophones

In English, many words sound the same but are spelled differently and have different meanings. These are called homophones. You can use the context of a sentence to decide which word is appropriate to use. **Circle the correct word.**

1. The doctor exhibited extreme (patients, patience) with his many (patients, patience).
2. We were (peeling, pealing) apples as the bells started to (peel, peal).
3. He hung his shirt on the (hanger , hangar) that he found in the airplane (hanger, hangar).
4. The (least, leased) of his worries was the property he had (least, leased).
5. This (mourning, morning) we are (mourning, morning) the loss of our pet.
6. Jamison's arms were (soar, sore) as he watched his kite (soar, sore) over the field.
7. He used his (bare, bear) hands to fight the big grizzly (bare, bear).
8. Laura used (tax, tacks) to put the (tax, tacks) flyer on the bulletin board.
9. The older man shook his (grayed, grade) head at the student's (grayed , grade).
10. Makayla (adds, ads) information to the newspaper (adds, ads).
11. You (need, knead) strong hands to (need, knead) that dough.
12. The bus (fare, fair) was $3.00 in order to get to the county (fare, fair).

Indirect Object

If a direct object is the object of the action of the verb, what is an indirect object? The direct object answers the question "what?" The indirect object answers the question "to whom or for whom?" It is the noun or pronoun that is indirectly affected by the action of a verb.

In the sentence: **Bill played his grandmother a piece on his guitar.** Bill is the subject and played is the verb. He played what? A piece. He played for whom? His grandmother. Therefore, piece is the direct object and grandmother is the indirect object.

Note that if you use the word "for," as in "He played the guitar for his grandmother," grandmother is now the object of the preposition for, but is still the indirect object of the sentence. Find the indirect object in each sentence.

1. Savannah told her grandmother the speech she was planning to make.
2. Tell your sister that you are sorry you yelled at her.
3. The boss offered Julio a raise.
4. The captain gave the crew very distinct orders.
5. Would you please give me some water?
6. The grateful couple took the nurses a batch of cookies.
7. Could you show Paula the playground?
8. It would be good to serve the patrons their dinners now.
9. Did you give the horses enough food and water?
10. Thomas gave Christine the answers to the test.

SELF DISCIPLINE - Kristi Yamaguchi

In 1992, Kristi won an Olympic Gold medal - the first American woman to win the Olympics in figure skating since 1976.

Kristi Yamaguchi grew up in Fremont, California. She was born with a clubfoot. Some children are treated with surgery. Others, like Kristi, wear heavy casts and undergo physical therapy to straighten the foot.

As a little girl, Kristi watched her big sister Lori ice skate, so of course she wanted to try. Skating was also recommended as physical therapy for her. She practiced before and after school and worked hard to do well at skating as well as in school.

After Kristi Yamaguchi's Olympic gold medal in 1992, she continued to compete as a professional skater.

Kristi founded the Always Dream Foundation in 1996. The mission of the foundation is to encourage and support the hopes and dreams of children. One project of her foundation is building playgrounds where children of all abilities can play together. She is determined to make a positive difference in children's lives.

In 2008, Kristi took on a new challenge as a contestant on Dancing with the Stars. She practiced for several months for up to six hours a day with her partner Mark Ballas in order to break what she called bad ice skating habits. She and her partner won the 6th season championship of Dancing with the Stars. Kristi continues to demonstrate that self-discipline can lead to achievement of your goals.

1. How was Kristi's self discipline in skating different from dancing? _____
   _____

2. How was Kristi's self discipline in skating the same as in dancing? _____
   _____

3. What is special about the playgrounds Kristi's foundation designs? _____
   _____

4. What are two reasons Kristi took up skating? _____
   _____
   _____

Color a star for each time you show Self-Discipline through your own actions this week.

Write a 50-75 word essay describing one of your Self-Discipline actions this week.

Self-Discipline – Memorize Your Value

"In reading the lives of great men, I found that the first victory they won was over themselves...self discipline with all of them came first."

– Harry S. Truman

Core Value Booklist
Read More About Self Discipline

Hatchet
by Gary Paulsen

Beyond the Divide
by Kathryn Lasky

The Dram Road
by Louise Lawrence

Touching Spirit Bear
by Ben Mikaelsen

Runaway
by Wendelin Van Draanen

..........TECH TIME!..........

As you have learned, self- discipline is an important part of being successful. Using a web 2.0 tool linked from our website or that you find on your own, create a mind map about at least 3 qualities of self- discipline you have and at least 3 areas of self- discipline you can improve on.

www.SummerFitLearning.com

Bill Gates
Tech Guru and
Philanthropist
gatesfoundation.org

Play Time!

Choose a Game or Activity to Play for 60 minutes today!

YOU CHOOSE

_____

Write down which game or activity you played today!

 Be Healthy! Instead of playing a video game play a board game.

DAY 5

WEEK 4

1 2 3 4

PARENT TIPS FOR WEEK 5

Skills of the Week

✔ Equations: 1 and 2 variables
✔ Volcanoes
✔ Setting: time
✔ Europe
✔ Spelling
✔ Coordinates on a quadrant plane
✔ Plate tectonics
✔ Mood
✔ Proofreading
✔ Commission
✔ Africa
✔ Personification
✔ Demonstrative adjectives

Weekly Value Kindness

Pelé

Kindness is caring about people, animals and the earth. It is looking for ways to help others.

Being nice to others catches on. When people are nice to each other they feel better about themselves and others. Small things make a big difference so when you smile, lend a helping hand and show concern for others, you are making the world a better place.

Stretching is Very Important
Get into the habit of stretching every night before you go to bed, as well as before you exercise every day.

Play 60 Every Day!

Run, jump, dance and have fun outside every day for 60 minutes!

Health and Wellness

Acne: those are the red bumps called pimples that a lot of kids and teenagers get on their skin. It is very common. Makes sure to drink plenty of water and wash your face with a gentle face cleanser every day. No picking at them, it makes them worse!

WEEK 5

Check the ☑ As You Complete Your Daily Task

	Day 1	Day 2	Day 3	Day 4	Day 5
MIND	☐	☐	☐	☐	☐
BODY	☐	☐	☐	☐	☐
DAILY READING	☐ 30 minutes	☐ 30 minutes	☐ 30 minutes	☐ 30 minutes	☐ 30 minutes

"I am kind"

_____

Print Name

Solve simple equations with 1 variable

If the same quantity is added to or subtracted from both sides of an equation, the two sides of the equation remain in balance. If both sides of an equation are multiplied or divided by the same number, the two sides of the equation remain in balance. The answer is obtained when only the variable exists on one side.

Example: Equation : $3y + 34 = 2y + 89$
Subtract 34 from both sides : $3y + 34 - 34 = 2y + 89 - 34$
Simplification gives : $3y = 2y + 55$
Subtract 2y from both sides: $3y - 2y = 2y - 2y + 55$
Answer : $y = 55$

1. $5z + 97 = 3z + 33$

3. $5a + 17 = 2a + 50$

2. $3a - 14 = 18 - a$

4. $5a - 28 = 72 + a$

DAY
1

2

3

4

5

WEEK 5

Volcanoes

A volcano is a mountain that opens downward to a pool of molten rock below the surface of the earth. When pressure builds up, eruptions occur. Gases and rock shoot up through the opening and spill over or fill the air with lava fragments. Eruptions can cause lava flows, hot ash flows, mudslides, avalanches, falling ash and floods. Volcano eruptions have been known to knock down entire forests. An erupting volcano can trigger tsunamis, flash floods, earthquakes, mudflows and rockfalls.

Volcanoes are formed when magma from within the Earth's upper mantle works its way to the surface. At the surface, it erupts to form lava flows and ash deposits. Over time as the volcano continues to erupt, it will get bigger and bigger.

There are more than 1500 active volcanoes on the Earth. We currently know of 80 or more under the oceans. Active volcanoes in the U.S. are found mainly in Hawaii, Alaska, California, Oregon and Washington.

1. What part of the United States seems to have most active volcanoes?

A) the east coast   B) the south   C) the west coast   D) the Great Plains

2. Volcanoes can

A) trigger tsunamis   B) create sinkholes   C) bring rain   D) none of these

3. What, in your opinion, is the most dangerous effect of a volcano?

_____

_____

_____

Aerobic

Go to www.summerfitlearning.com for more Activities!

DAILY EXERCISE
Jogging for Fitness 10
"Stretch Before You Play!"

Instruction
Jog 10 minutes in
place or outside

Be Healthy!
Stretch before
you exercise
to help avoid
injury.

DAY 1

2

3

4

5

WEEK 5

Setting - Time

The setting of a story, poem, or play is the time and place of the action. Elements of setting may include geographic location, historical period (past, present, or future), the season of the year, the time of day, and the culture of a society. The influence of setting on characters' decisions and actions may vary in different stories. Setting can help determine what happens to the characters and how they resolve their problems.

Consider the following setting: The year is 1935. The place is a cabin in a remote forest in northern Montana. The closest town is 45 miles away. The season is mid-winter. It is cold and there is a possibility of snow. Six couples have gathered in this out of the way spot to celebrate New Years Eve.

In this time period, there were no cell phones, and remote areas didn't have phone lines to houses or cabins. Roads in remote areas were poorly constructed and poorly kept up. Cars were not as fast as today; most in town speed limits were around 25 miles per hour. Out in the country, a person could probably drive as fast as they wanted, which was probably around 50-60 miles per hour. There was no such thing as central heating; in all likelihood, warmth would have been generated by fireplaces. In a remote area there would have been no electricity.

Determine whether each statement below is true or false.

1. _____ These people could enjoy a lovely holiday celebration together.

2. _____ In case of emergency, the people could contact a hospital or police easily.

3. _____ The people do not face a danger of becoming stranded at the cabin.

4. _____ If a snowstorm hit, the people could be stranded in the cabin for several days.

5. _____ One of the conflicts that could be probable is some of the people deciding to have a car race.

6. _____ One of the conflicts that could be probable is someone getting lost in the forest while gathering wood for the fire.

If you were told to find 3 different solutions for the equation $x + y = 10$, you could put any number in the equation for either x or y, and solve for the other variable. If $x = 4$, y must be 6. If $y = 3$, x must be 7. If $x = -1$, then $y = 11$.

You could also be given an ordered pair (3, 7) where the first number replaces x and the second number replaces y. You would put those two numbers into the equation, to see if that is a possible solution.

1. Does the ordered pair (4, 5) solve the equation $3x + y = 17$? _____

2. Does the ordered pair (5, 2) solve the equation $3x + y = 17$? _____

3. Does the ordered pair (3, 2) solve the equation $3x + y = 17$? _____

4. Does the ordered pair (7, -4) solve the equation $3x + y = 17$? _____

5. Does the ordered pair (-4, 7) solve the equation $3x + y = 17$? _____

Europe

Europe is the sixth largest continent in size and the third largest in population. It is bordered by the Mediterranean Sea to the south, Asia to the east, and the Atlantic Ocean to the West. Europe is a wealthy continent and is the center of the West and Western Democracy.

Russia is considered to be part of both Europe and Asia. The area of Russia that is west of the Ural Mountains is usually considered part of Europe. The tallest mountain in Europe is Mount Elbrus in Russia. Europe has been the home to some of the Earth's greatest civilizations from Ancient Greece to the Roman Empire. It is also the home to the birth of democracy. Europe has been the central point of two of the biggest wars in modern history: World War I and World War II. Recently Europe has united under the common union called the European Union. This union allows independent European countries to have a single currency and to combine their economic and military power. Most of Europe now uses the same currency called the Euro.

Europe is the home to many of the world's oldest countries including the 5 oldest; San Marino, France, Bulgaria, Denmark, and Portugal. It is also home to the smallest country in the world, the Holy See or the Vatican. It is the smallest country both in size and population.

1. What is the currency which is now used by most European countries?

_____

2. Which country is considered part of both Europe and Asia? _____

3. Why do we say Europe is home to the birth of democracy? _____

_____

Strength

Go to www.summerfitlearning.com for more Activities!

DAILY EXERCISE
Chin-ups
"Stretch Before You Play!"

Instruction
Repeat 2 times

Be Healthy!
Stop eating when you are full.

1

DAY 2

3

4

5

W E E K 5

Mood

Mood is the general atmosphere created by the author's words. It is the feeling the reader gets from reading those words. It is the emotions that you (the reader) feel while you are reading. Some literature makes you feel sad, others joyful, still others, angry. **Read the following poem.**

The Raven by Edgar Allen Poe

Once upon a midnight dreary, while I pondered, weak and weary,
Over many a quaint and curious volume of forgotten lore,
While I nodded, nearly napping, suddenly there came a tapping,
As of some one gently rapping, rapping at my chamber door.
"'Tis some visitor," I muttered, "tapping at my chamber door -
Only this, and nothing more."

Ah, distinctly I remember it was in the bleak December,
And each separate dying ember wrought its ghost upon the floor.
Eagerly I wished the morrow; - vainly I had sought to borrow
From my books surcease of sorrow - sorrow for the lost Lenore -
For the rare and radiant maiden whom the angels name Lenore -
Nameless here for evermore.

1. Would you say the mood of this poem is angry, happy, or gloomy? _____

2. What words in the first line set the mood?_____
_____

3. There is some repetition in the first stanza, which perhaps changes the mood to a little

anxious. What are the repeated words? _____
_____

4. Remember that alliteration is the repetition of a particular sound in the first syllables of a

series of words or phrases. What words in line eleven are an example of alliteration?

_____

5. What does the author imply has happened to Lenore? _____

_____

Mark the correct place on the quadrant plane

A (-3 2)

B (-2, -2)

C (5, 3)

D (2, -3)

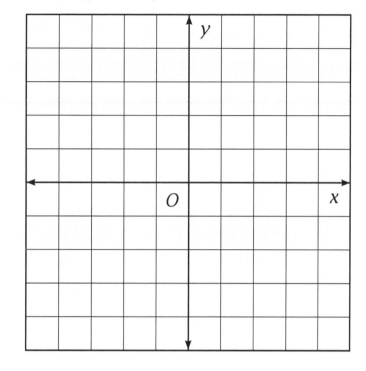

Plate Tectonics

There are eight major plates on the earth's surface and many minor plates. They are constantly moving, though generally only a few centimeters a year. The plates are drifting on top of the soft mantle layer. They can move horizontally or vertically. They may change in size as edges are built up, crushed together, or pushed back into the mantle.

When the plates run into each other, or slide under each other, it causes earthquakes and volcanoes, and sometimes huge mountain chains, like the Alps or the Himalayas, get pushed up high above sea level.

The landmasses are still moving today. North America and South America are gradually moving away from Europe and Africa, so that the Atlantic Ocean is getting bigger and the Pacific Ocean is getting smaller. The California edge of the Pacific Ocean is ramming into North America and sliding past it, causing earthquakes in California and building up the Rocky Mountains. In several hundred million years, the Pacific Ocean will probably disappear, and the West Coast of North America will smash into Japan and China.

Unscramble the words found in the information above.

1. _____ eteicmtsner

2. _____ razhioonlytl

3. _____ ricetlavly

4. _____ iiapcfc

5. _____ aructqaheks

6. _____ loavsocn

DAY 3

WEEK 5

DAILY EXERCISE
Speed
"Stretch Before You Play!"

Instruction
Run 3 Blocks

Be Healthy!
Wash fruits and vegetables before eating them.

1

2

DAY 3

4

5

W E E K 5

Proofread/correct

An important skill for writing is proofreading. This involves checking for several things: correct spelling, correct punctuation, proper word choice, and correct grammar. Check the paragraph below. Underline letters that need to be capitalized. Put in punctuation marks where needed. Write correct spelling above misspelled words. Write corrected grammar above incorrect words. Cross out punctuation which is not needed.

Joseph and Helen were going on a picnic. They was happy to be getting away from school and work for awhile. Helen paked a great picnic basket. Joseph had helpped, her to make several kinds of sandwhiches. They had put in some chips, soda, napkins, and, paper plates. They even have some fudge for desert. When they got everything ready, they headed for the door. But two their dismay, the overcast sky began to drip raindrops on everything. At first, Joseph and Helen were disappointed, but then they thinked, they could still have the picnic – on the living room floor! It was a great picnic?

Spelling
Choose the word in each group which is incorrectly spelled.

1.	chief	captain	curtain	pleassure
2.	dollars	instaed	forty	cough
3.	contain	greif	laugh	weight
4.	amoung	pitcher	station	though
5.	whisper	complaint	reletive	importance
6.	repair	caried	vacation	twelve
7,	apoint	famous	either	dangerous
8.	primary	different	canvas	soldire
9.	entertain	purpose	diamand	neighbor
10.	patient	tomato	advize	whistle
11.	arguement	saucer	recess	college
12.	therefore	anxious	purchase	amusment
13.	solemn	atorney	agreement	mosquito
14.	citizen	exceptions	eleberate	welfare

Calculate commission

Many people work in a job where they work on commission. That is, they earn a percentage of the price of the item they sell. This is a real life usage of percent. For example, Miles is a car salesman. He earns a salary, but he also gets a 3% commission on every car he sells. To calculate this, change the percent to a decimal and multiply. If he sells a car for $17,500, when you multiply $17,500 by 0.03, his commission is $525.

1. Angela is an art dealer. She earns 15% on each painting she sells. She sold 3 paintings this week for $825 each. How much commission did she earn?

_____

2. Pierre is an agent for actors. He earns 10% of his clients' salaries. If his clients earned $42,654 this month, what is Pierre's commission?

_____

3. JoAnne sells real estate. This month she earned $10, 413 in commission on the properties she sold for $80,100. What percent commission does she charge?

_____

Personification

Personification is a figure of speech (generally considered a type of metaphor) in which an inanimate object or abstraction is given human qualities or abilities. This is done very frequently in poetry, but is also found in prose. An example is "Justice is blind and, at times, deaf." Justice, an abstract quality, is given the human traits of being blind and deaf. The meaning is that justice should be meted out according to the law only, not to what influences us by sight and sound.

In the following sentences, underline the word which is being personified and the human quality or trait being used.

1. The sorry engine wheezed its death cough.
2. The pizza Jasmine had eaten was having an argument with her stomach.
3. The candle flame danced in the darkened hallway.
4. Light had conquered the darkness.
5. After Michelle left, the party died.
6. Winter's icy grip held on tightly to the March days.
7. Las Vegas has been called the city that never sleeps.
8. The birds played hide and seek in the corn fields.
9. The first rays of sunlight sneaked in under the curtains.
10. The wind sang its sad song through the dark trees.
11. The sun was glaring down on the desert with a fierce intensity.
12. The warm wind wrapped its arms around the small child.
13. The ancient door squeaked a protest as it was slowly opened.
14. The flowers bent their heads is sorrow as the sun left the sky.
15. The chocolate éclairs called to me from across the room.

DAILY EXERCISE
Heel Raises
"Stretch Before You Play!"

Instruction
Repeat 8 times

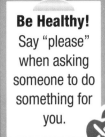

Be Healthy!
Say "please" when asking someone to do something for you.

Demonstrative adjectives

In English the demonstrative adjectives are used to indicate specific items in relation to ourselves. To indicate a specific shirt that I want you to look at, I will point to the shirt and ask "What do you think of this shirt?" And you might reply, "I don't like that shirt."

The demonstrative adjectives are: **this, that, these, those, this one** and **that one**. We never use "this here" or "that there," though we might say "this one here" or "that one there."

Choose the correct demonstrative adjective for each sentence.

1. Don't do it like that, do it _____ way.
2. Take one of _____ pencils from that basket.
3. Everyone rode a horse in _____ days.
4. I'm going on a trip _____ Friday.
5. Could you bring me _____ scissors I left in the other room?
6. I've got to solve _____ math problems before I can play.
7. _____ are my paintings on the wall here.
8. _____ are Jeremy's paintings on the wall over there.
9. _____ book you are reading looks very interesting.
10. _____ table over there has a broken leg.

Africa

The continent of Africa borders the southern half of the Mediterranean Sea. The Atlantic Ocean is to the west and the Indian Ocean is to the Southeast. Africa stretches well south of the equator and covers more than 12 million square miles. Africa is the world's second largest continent and is also the world's second most populous continent.

Africa is one of the most diverse places on the planet. Climates range from deserts to tropical jungles and rain forests. There are mountains, savannahs, rivers, and lakes. Africa is home to a huge variety of animals, including elephants, giraffes, gorillas, hippopotamus, cheetahs, rhinoceros, monkeys, lions and zebras.

The highest point in Africa is Mount Kilimanjaro in Tanzania at 5895 meters high. The lowest point is Lake Asal in Djibouti at 153 meters below sea level. The largest country in Africa is Sudan; the smallest is the Seychelles. The most populated country is Nigeria and the largest city is Cairo in Egypt. The largest lake in Africa is Lake Victoria and the longest river is The Nile River which is also the longest river in the world. African languages are varied with more than 1000 languages spoken across the continent.

Unscramble the words below that are from this selection.

1. virsede _____
2. soupoulp _____
3. inalkimajor _____
4. torvaici _____
5. diranemeteran _____
6. upopostihpam _____
7. sorinechor _____
8. havannas _____

KINDNESS – Pele

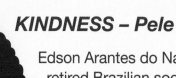

Edson Arantes do Nascimento, better known as Pelé is a retired Brazilian soccer player. He is widely regarded as the best to ever play the game. He began playing for an area minor league club as a teenager.

Pele was raised in a very poor family. As a teenager, when he wasn't playing soccer, he was shining shoes for pennies.

At 17, Pele scored two goals in a championship game to help Brazil win its first World Cup. Pele played in four World Cups with Brazil's National Team. During his career he scored 1,280 goals in 1,360 games.

Pelé is an icon in Brazil and around the world. He has worked for children's causes through UNICEF. He has been a patron of the ABC Trust since 2002 and has donated a number of signed items. The ABC Trust 'Action for Brazil's Children' is a United Kingdom based charity that is dedicated to helping street children and the most vulnerable young people of Brazil. By raising funding and awareness, they support local community-led organizations in Brazil which give these children the support, education and inspiration they need to transform their own futures.

He also supports Great Ormond Street Hospital in London. They treat children who are suffering from the rarest, most complex and often life-threatening conditions.

His good works are not limited to Brazil and England. He supports The Littlest Lamb, which is a non-profit organization dedicated to providing a safe, loving and supportive home for children who have lost one or both parents. They are currently building an orphanage in Egypt.

1. What is a synonym for transform? _____

2. Pele's charity work seems to be focused on what group of people? _____

_____

3. What facility is the Littlest Lamb building in Egypt? _____

_____

4. Based on the story, why might Pele be interested in helping children? _____

_____

_____

_____

Color a star for each time you show Kindness through your own actions this week.

 Write a 50-75 word essay describing one of your Kindness actions this week.

Kindness – Memorize Your Value

"How lovely to think that no one need wait a moment. We can start now, start slowly, changing the world. How lovely that everyone, great and small, can make a contribution toward introducing justice straightaway. And you can always, always give something, even if it is only kindness!"

– Anne Frank

Core Value Booklist
Read More About Kindness

Somebody Everybody Listens To
by Suzanne Supplee

Ruined
by Paula Morris

The Terrible Wave
by Marden Dahlstedt

Jane Addams
by Mary Kittredge

Their House
by Mary Towne

.........TECH TIME!.........

You can tell people what you think, what you want, and what you believe is important through posters. Making posters with a web 2.0 tool can be fun. Many sites will allow you to choose from a variety of poster templates. Create a poster that shows what you learned about Pelé and kindness. Share your poster with friends or family and enjoy the fun together!

www.SummerFitLearning.com

Bill Gates
Tech Guru and Philanthropist
gatesfoundation.org

Play Time!
Choose a Game or Activity to Play for 60 minutes today!

YOU CHOOSE

_____

Write down which game or activity you played today!

Be Healthy!
Eat all your meals at the kitchen table today.

76   © Summer Fit

WEEK 6

Skills of the Week

- ✔ Percent of increase or decrease
- ✔ Asia
- ✔ Hyperbole
- ✔ Additive and multiplicative inverse
- ✔ Summary
- ✔ Irregular verbs
- ✔ Commutative property and additive inverse
- ✔ South America
- ✔ Distributive property and additive inverse
- ✔ Metamorphic rocks
- ✔ Comprehension
- ✔ Spelling
- ✔ North America
- ✔ Semicolons

Weekly Value Courage

Teddy Draper Sr.

Courage means doing the right thing even when it is difficult and you are afraid. It means to be brave.

It can be a lot easier to do the right thing when everybody else is doing it, but it can be a lot harder to do it on our own or when nobody is looking. Remember who you are and stand up for what you believe in when it is easy and even more so when it is hard.

Stretching is Very Important
Get into the habit of stretching every night before you go to bed, as well as before you exercise every day.

Play 60 Every Day!
Run, jump, dance and have fun outside every day for 60 minutes!

Health and Wellness

Protect your great smile:)! Brush, floss and get your dental checkups.

WEEK 6

Check the ✓ As You Complete Your Daily Task

	Day 1	Day 2	Day 3	Day 4	Day 5
MIND	☐	☐	☐	☐	☐
BODY	☐	☐	☐	☐	☐
DAILY READING	☐ 30 minutes	☐ 30 minutes	☐ 30 minutes	☐ 30 minutes	☐ 30 minutes

"I am brave"

_____

Print Name

Calculate percent of increase or decrease

When a quantity grows (gets bigger), then we can compute its PERCENT INCREASE:

PERCENT INCREASE = (new amount–original amount) ÷ original amount. The answer will be in the form of a decimal, which we know how to change to a percent (multiply by 100)
When a quantity shrinks (gets smaller), then we can compute its PERCENT DECREASE:

PERCENT DECREASE = (original amount–new amount) ÷ original amount, multiplied by 100 to be in the form of a percent.

1. Jacques had 25 cars on his lot, now he has 10. What is the percent of decrease?

_____

2) Marcy started with 12 pairs of shoes, now she has 20. What is the percent of increase?

_____

DAY
1

2

3

4

5

WEEK 6

Asia

The continent of Asia is the world's largest and most populous continent. Over 4 billion people live in Asia. Asia also contains the world's most populous country, China, and the world's largest country, Russia. Asia borders Africa and Europe to the west and the Pacific Ocean to the east.

The continent of Asia is so large and diverse that it often is divided into sub-regions: Northern Asia, Middle East, Southern Asia, Eastern Asia, Southeastern Asia. Asia is rich in diverse races, cultures, and languages. Many of the world's major religions came out of Asia including Christianity, Judaism, Islam, Hinduism, and Buddhism.

Countries such as Russia, China, Japan and India produce products and services that are used by every nation in the world. Asia is also abundant in natural resources. Oil in the Middle East is a major supplier of much of the world's energy. This means that Asia has a major influence on the world's economy.

The highest point on earth, Mt. Everest, is in Asia. The lowest point on land, the Dead Sea, is also in Asia.   Asia is the only continent that shares borders with two other continents; Africa and Europe.

1. Asia is connected to which other continents?_____

_____

2. What is the world's most populous country? _____

3. How does the size of Asia affect its diversity? _____

_____

_____

Aerobic Go to www.summerfitlearning.com for more Activities!

DAILY EXERCISE
Pass and Go
"Stretch Before You Play!"

Instruction
Get a Friend to Play this Game With You!

Be Healthy!
Ask your parents if you can do something for them.

DAY 1

2

3

4

5

WEEK 6

Hyperbole

A **hyperbole** (pronounced hi-per-bo-lee) is an exaggerated statement or figure of speech not intended to be taken literally, such as "to wait an eternity." Some other common examples are:

> They ran like greased lightning.
> He's got tons of money.
> Her brain is the size of a pea.
> He is older than the hills.
> I will die if she asks me to dance.
> That cat is as big as an elephant!
> I'm so hungry I could eat a horse.
> I have told you a million times not to lie!

As you can see, often the hyperbole is given in the form of a simile or metaphor. Practice your own skills here. Think of an outrageous example for each of the ideas below.

1. Her eyes were as big as _____

2. He was as curious as _____

3. The thunder was as loud as _____

4. The treasure was as fantastic as _____

5. The children ran like _____

6. You snore louder than _____

7. My backpack weighs as much as _____

8. That guy is as tall as _____

In the last examples, explain what is meant by the exaggeration.

9. My feet were killing me. _____

10. I was so tired I couldn't move. _____

11. My computer is older than the dinosaurs. _____

12. Jacqui will be back in a second. _____

80 © Summer Fit

The **additive inverse** is the number you add to another number to get zero. The additive inverse of 5 is -5; the inverse of -5 is 5. The multiplicative inverse is the number you multiply to get 1. The multiplicative inverse of 2 is ½. We use these inverses when solving equations in order to isolate the unknown on one side of the equation.

Find the additive and the multiplicative inverses for each number.

1. 17 _____ additive inverse _____ multiplicative inverse

2. -32 _____ additive inverse _____ multiplicative inverse

3. 1/4 _____ additive inverse _____ multiplicative inverse

4. 3/5 _____ additive inverse _____ multiplicative inverse

5. 7/10 _____ additive inverse _____ multiplicative inverse

Summary

A summary is a condensed version of a larger reading. A summary is not a rewrite of the original piece and should not be long. To write a summary, use your own words to express the main idea briefly and give important details of the piece you have read. Your purpose in writing the summary is to give the basic ideas of the original reading. What was it about and what did the author want to communicate? Who were the major characters and what conflict did they face? What were the major plot complications? How was the conflict resolved?

Choose a book you have read in the past year. Write a summary of at least 10 sentences. Be sure to cover the major plot points. Check your work for spelling and grammar correctness.

_____

_____

_____

_____

_____

_____

_____

_____

DAY 2

3

4

5

WEEK 6

Strength Go to www.summerfitlearning.com for more Activities!

DAILY EXERCISE
Squats
"Stretch Before You Play!"

Instruction
Repeat 6 Times

Be Healthy!
Everybody gets bad breath, so remember to brush your teeth!

Irregular Verbs

Regular verbs change their form very little. The past tense and the past participle of regular verbs end in –ed, for example: play, played, played. Irregular verbs, however, as their name suggests, do not follow a regular pattern. Over time, we just have to learn what the correct form of the verb is.

In the chart below, fill in the correct missing form for each verb. The first one is done for you.

Present tense	Past tense	Past participle
Arise	Arose	Arisen
Begin	1.	Begun
Grow	Grew	2.
3.	Rode	Ridden
Speak	4.	Spoken
5.	Found	Found
Get	6.	Gotten
Ring	Rang	7.
Throw	8.	Thrown
9.	Wrote	Written
Forgive	Forgave	10.

The commutative property means that addends can be added in any order and the sum will be the same. This works with subtraction because you can change the number being subtracted to its inverse and add it. So, $3 - 2 + 7 = 3 + 7 + (-2) = 10 + (-2) = 8$.

Solve these equations.

1. $23 + 17 + 77 =$ _____

2. $-9 + 50 + 14 - 5 =$ _____

3. $7 + 22 + 13 + 8 =$ _____

4. $19 - 1 + 11 - 6 =$ _____

5. $100 - 25 + 5 - 25 =$ _____

6. $-2 + 8 + 2 =$ _____

7. $17 - 6 + 36 =$ _____

8. $50 - 3 + 5 - 7 =$ _____

9. $-14 + 22 + 12 - 0 =$ _____

10. $63 + 14 + 7 + 6 =$ _____

Comprehension

An excerpt from *Treasure Island* by Robert Lewis Stevenson

It was not very long after this that there occurred the first of the mysterious events that rid us at last of the captain, though not, as you will see, of his affairs. It was a bitter cold winter, with long, hard frosts and heavy gales; and it was plain from the first that my poor father was little likely to see the spring. He sank daily, and my mother and I had all the inn upon our hands, and were kept busy enough without paying much regard to our unpleasant guest.

It was one January morning, very early--a pinching, frosty morning--the cove all grey with hoar-frost, the ripple lapping softly on the stones, the sun still low and only touching the hilltops and shining far to seaward. The captain had risen earlier than usual and set out down the beach, his cutlass swinging under the broad skirts of the old blue coat, his brass telescope under his arm, his hat tilted back upon his head. I remember his breath hanging like smoke in his wake as he strode off, and the last sound I heard of him as he turned the big rock was a loud snort of indignation, as though his mind was still running upon Dr. Livesey.

Well, mother was upstairs with father and I was laying the breakfast-table against the captain's return when the parlour door opened and a man stepped in on whom I had never set my eyes before. He was a pale, tallowy creature, wanting two fingers of the left hand, and though he wore a cutlass, he did not look much like a fighter. I had always my eye open for seafaring men, with one leg or two, and I remember this one puzzled me. He was not sailorly, and yet he had a smack of the sea about him too.

1. What is meant by "my poor father was little likely to see the spring"? _____

_____

2. What was the temperature like on the morning in the story? _____

_____

3. Where had the captain gone on his walk? _____

4. What is meant by "wanting two fingers on the left hand"? _____

_____

5. What seems to be the boy's impression of the captain? _____

_____

6. What evidence supports your answer? _____

_____

Side tabs: 1 2 DAY 3 4 5 WEEK 6

Aerobic Go to www.summerfitlearning.com for more Activities!

DAILY EXERCISE
Capture the Flag
"Stretch Before You Play!"

Instruction
Get Your Family and Friends to Play

Be Healthy!
Ask your parents to buy 1% or skim milk instead of whole milk.

1
2
DAY 3
4
5

WEEK 6

South America

South America is the fourth largest continent in size and the fifth largest in population. It is located primarily in the southern hemisphere. It is bordered by the Atlantic Ocean to the east and the Pacific Ocean to the west. The Andes Mountain Range and the Amazon River (second longest river in the world) are the major landforms in South America. The Amazon River basin and rain forest is home to some of the world's most unique animals and plants. There are over 2000 species of butterflies there!

Before European colonization, the Incan Civilization was the strongest force in South America. Then Spain and Portugal colonized much of South America. The colonies gained independence in the 1800's with the help of leaders such as Simon Bolivar and Jose de San Martin. Much of South America still speaks Spanish and the primary language of Brazil is Portuguese.

The highest point in South America is Cerro Aconcagua in the Andes Mountains in the country of Argentina. The largest South American country in both size and population is Brazil. The largest city is Sao Paulo, Brazil, which is also one of the ten largest cities in the world. The highest waterfall in the world is Santo del Angel (also called Angel Falls). It is almost 1000 meters high!

1. What is important about the Amazon Rain Forest? _____
_____

2. What civilization was a strong force before European colonization? _____
_____

Semicolons

A semicolon is usually used to connect two independent clauses, or sentences, that are closely related. It can also be used to separate a list of items which use other punctuation, such as commas.

Place the semicolon in the correct place in each sentence.

1. It is raining outside I will wear my raincoat today.
2. We are going swimming tomorrow we are going out for dinner afterwards.
3. I would love to go to Italy Rome has such interesting history.
4. Patrick recently took up the drums I pity his neighbors.
5. I had a busy evening I played cards, read a bit and watched TV.
6. Next month I am going on a trip I need to go visit my grandmother.
7. She loves The Beatles she knows every song by heart.
8. The artist preferred to work in watercolors he did not like pastels.
9. Clarise was late for class again she will have to serve detention now.
10. Some people love chocolate cake some prefer apple pie.

Using the Distributive Property and Additive inverse

The Distributive Property is easy to remember, if you recall that "multiplication *distributes* over addition." Formally, they write this property as "a(b + c) = ab + ac." In numbers, this means, that 2(3 + 4) = 2×3 + 2×4. This works with subtraction as well if we remember that subtracting a number is the same as adding a negative number. Therefore 4x-12 = 4 (x – 3). We can use this property to multiply mentally.

Example: 7 x 68 = (7 x 60) + (7 x 8) = 420 + 56 = 476. This property can also help solve simple algebraic equations. 6 (2x +3) = 42; 12x + 18 = 42; 12x +18 – 18 = 42 – 18; 12 x = 24; 12x ÷12 = 24 ÷ 12; x = 2.

1. x + 9 = 18 - 2x _____

2. 2 (x - 6) = 18 _____

3. -32 = 4(x + 3) _____

4. 3x (3 + 5) = 24 _____

5. 8 (x + 1) = 48 _____

6. 5 (14 – x) = 60 _____

7. 3 (x + 5) = 21 _____

8. 9 (2 + x) = 63 _____

9. 2 (x + 1) = x + 5 _____

10. 4 (x - 3) = 23 - x _____

Metamorphic Rock

Metamorphic rocks are rocks that were once igneous or sedimentary rocks and have morphed (changed) into something else. They form deep within the earth when heat and pressure are applied to the original rocks. The heat and pressure "cook" the rocks, changing their structure. The rocks are melted partially. The chemicals in them are rearranged so the final rock is different from the original one. Most of the rocks that form the continental land mass are metamorphic. There are three ways the metamorphism takes place.

The first kind of metamorphism is rocks simply getting buried by new rocks. The weight from the top rocks forces them deeper in the earth and exposes them to more heat. This is the most common type of metamorphism. Another way metamorphic rocks are formed is contact metamorphism. Magma may push its way up through the crust along cracks in the earth. As the magma cools, it forms igneous rock. The rock touched by the magma can be changed by the magma's heat and pressure from surrounding rock and become metamorphic. The third process to form metamorphic rock is a tectonic process. When tectonic plates move along and past one another, they sometimes push very hard or crash against each other. The heat and pressure caused by this process can cause metamorphosis.

1. What are the two basic elements for rocks to become metamorphic? _____

_____

_____

2. What in the rock changes so that it becomes a different rock? _____

_____

DAILY EXERCISE
Lunges
"Stretch Before You Play!"

Instruction
Repeat 5 times with each leg

Be Healthy!
Drinking soda can add unhealthy fat to your body.

1
2
3
DAY 4
5

WEEK 6

North America

North America extends from just north of the equator to the Arctic Ocean. North America is the third largest continent. It is bordered by the Atlantic Ocean to the east and the Pacific Ocean to the west. North America is dominated by its three largest countries: Canada, Mexico, and the United States. Central America and the Caribbean are usually considered part of North America as well. There are 32 countries in those areas.

Before it was colonized, Central America was home to the Olmec, the Aztec and the Maya – all strong cultures which shaped the area of Central America, especially Mexico. The rest of North America was populated by thousands of Native American groups.

The majority of Central America was colonized by the Spanish. The United States was colonized by several European countries, but eventually most of those colonies were dominated by the English. Canada was a morsel fought over by France and England for many years, eventually to become part of the British Empire.

1. What are the three large countries in North America? _____

_____

2. Which country colonized most of Central America? _____

3. What language do you infer is spoken in most of Central America? _____

Spelling – Common mistakes
Correct the spelling of the bold word in each sentence.

1. _____ Bill Gates is a **successfull** business man.
2. _____ We are having a spell of warm **whether**.
3. _____ I am **sincerly** sorry that I have upset you.
4. _____ Many people are upset with the **goverment**.
5. _____ We are trying to keep the **enviroment** clean.
6. _____ His new jeans cost **fourty** dollars.
7. _____ Clara was definitely **suprised** that we threw her a party.
8. _____ Did you borrow these books from the **libary**?
9. _____ We had an **unforgetable** experience at the zoo.
10. _____ He learned a **valuble** lesson from his brother.
11. _____ Carmen tried to **embarass** her sister.
12. _____ I didn't **reconize** you without your glasses.
13. _____ His **apearance** was unexpected.
14. _____ His mother is a **proffessor** at the local college
15. _____ He went along his way quite **hapily**.

COURAGE – Teddy Draper Sr.

War very often gives us examples of courage. One group of men who demonstrated courage during World War II were the Navajo Code Talkers, and Teddy Draper Sr. was one of those men.

It was very important to be able to send messages in a code that the enemy could not break. This secrecy was crucial to saving the lives of our servicemen. It was discovered that the Navajo language was unbreakable. This code was said to be the reason for success of every major engagement of the Pacific, allowing troops to communicate quickly and securely. The code is credited with saving countless lives and helping to end the war.

When the Marines landed on Iwo Jima, Draper was wounded in his face and leg, but continued to fight. At one point he ran through heavy enemy fire and back to retrieve communication equipment which was necessary for the success of the battle.

When the Code Talkers returned home, they were told not to tell anyone of their top-secret mission. They were not recognized until 2001, when they were awarded Medals of Honor.

1. Define crucial: _____

2. Why would it be important to have an unbreakable code during wartime? _____

_____

_____

3. Find a word in the story that is a synonym for bring back. _____

4. Find a word in the story that is an antonym for failure. _____

5. Draw a picture of an award you would give to the Code Talkers.

Color a star for each time you show Courage through your own actions this week.

 Write a 50-75 word essay describing one of your Courage actions this week.

Courage – Memorize Your Value

"Courage is about doing what you're afraid to do. There can be no courage unless you're scared."

– Eddie Rickenbacker

Core Value Booklist
Read More About Courage

Alice the Brave
by Phyllis Reynolds Naylor

Red Cap
by G. Clifton Wisler

The Hero's Trail: A Guide for a Heroic Life
by T. A. Barron

When My Name Was Keoko
by Linda Sue Park

Steal Away
by Jennifer Armstrong

..........TECH TIME!..........

What does courage look like? Sometimes you need several different pictures to explain one word or idea. Creating a collage can allow you to express the meaning of one word in several different ways. Use your own photos or clipart on your computer to create a collage about courage. Find a web 2.0 tool that helps you do this online. See if your parent can guess the quality you are trying to show just by looking at your collage. Have your parent rate your success!

www.SummerFitLearning.com

Bill Gates
Tech Guru and Philanthropist
gatesfoundation.org

*Remember, web 2.0 tools are used to create and collaborate. So, share what you have done! Show your parents, guardian or friends and have them rate your project on this workbook page (provide a rating scale).

Play Time!
Choose a Game or Activity to Play for 60 minutes today!

YOU CHOOSE

_____
Write down which game or activity you played today!

Be Healthy!
Try to eat 3 different vegetables today!

1
2
3
4

DAY
5

WEEK 6

PARENT TIPS FOR WEEK 7

Skills of the Week

- ✔ Bar graphs, line graphs
- ✔ Earthquakes
- ✔ Word choice
- ✔ Colons
- ✔ Oceania
- ✔ Adjacent angles
- ✔ Sedimentary rocks
- ✔ Complimentary angles
- ✔ Economy
- ✔ Resolution
- ✔ Persuasive writing

Weekly Value Respect

The Dalai Lama

Respect is honoring yourself and others. It is behaving in a way that makes life peaceful and orderly.

Sometimes we forget to appreciate that every person is unique and different. All of us want to be accepted and appreciated for who we are. Try to treat others the way that you want to be treated, even when it is difficult.

Stretching is Very Important
Get into the habit of stretching every night before you go to bed, as well as before you exercise every day.

Play 60 Every Day!
Run, jump, dance and have fun outside every day for 60 minutes!

Health and Wellness

Find positive friends who can share and support your life goals. It is fun and important to be able to talk about your health and wellness with someone else.

Check the ✓ As You Complete Your Daily Task

	Day 1	Day 2	Day 3	Day 4	Day 5
MIND	☐	☐	☐	☐	☐
BODY	☐	☐	☐	☐	☐
DAILY READING	☐ 30 minutes	☐ 30 minutes	☐ 30 minutes	☐ 30 minutes	☐ 30 minutes

"I am respectful"

_____

Print Name

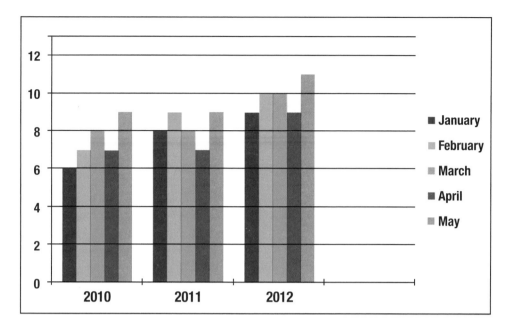

Pizzas (in thousands) delivered in Indianapolis, Indiana

1. In which year were more pizzas sold in April? _____

2. In which month and year were pizza sales the lowest? _____

3) In which month and year were pizza sales the highest? _____

4. What month and year matched the sales of January and March 2011? _____

How earthquakes are measured

The most common way earthquakes are measured is the Richter scale, from 1 to 10, developed by Charles Richter. He used a seismograph (a pendulum that records the tremors made by an earthquake) to record the severity of an earthquake. An earthquake measuring 5 on the Richter scale is 10 times stronger than an earthquake measuring 4 and a 6 is 10 times stronger than a 5. Earthquakes can be felt over large areas, but they usually last less than one minute. According to the U. S. Geological Survey, there are approximately 1,500,000 earthquakes a year. However, less than 2000 are greater than 5 on the Richter scale. Most earthquakes measure at 2 or lower and are barely felt by people. If you live in an area where earthquakes are common, it would be a good idea to have certain supplies available, whether you are at home or in a car.

Unscramble the words below to find what some of those suggested supplies are.

1. twear

2. klenbat

3. tliflashgh

4. tejakc

5. dirao

6. tebarites

Aerobic Go to www.summerfitlearning.com for more Activities!

DAILY EXERCISE
Mountain Climbers
"Stretch Before You Play!"

Instruction
Perform 3 x's for 60 seconds

Be Healthy!
Do not interrupt when someone is talking to you.

DAY 1

Word Choice

For an author, word choice is critical. Sometimes they are concerned about connotation and denotation. Other times an author is trying to create a certain mood or atmosphere with their word choice. Below is a poem which makes a joke about the spelling of the word llama. So he uses many words that contain one or more l's when correctly spelled. To add to the humor of the poem, he also used many "high-sounding" words – words that seem too fancy for the subject matter. He also uses at least one word not commonly used by most of us: infama. A yoke infama is an infamous or disgraceful harness worn by work animals.

Llyric of the LLama

Behold how from her lair the youthful llama
Llopes forth and llightly scans the llandscape o'er.
With llusty heart she llooks upon llife's drama,
Relying on her llate-llearnt worldly llore.

But llo! Some llad, armed with a yoke *infama*
Soon llures her into llowly llabor's cause;
Her wool is llopped to weave into pajama,
And llanguidly she llearns her Gees and Haws.

My children, heed this llesson from all llanguishing young lllamas,
If you would lllive with lllatitude, avoid each llluring lllay;
And do not llllightly lllleave, I beg, your llllonesome, lllloving mammas,
And llllast of allll, don't spelllll your name in such a sillllllly way.

– Burges Johnson, *Everybody's Magazine*, August 1907

1. In the first stanza, what is one word that perhaps seems "high-sounding" for this poem?

_____

2. In your own words, tell what the "llad" in the second stanza does. _____

_____

3. What word in stanza three means laying about weakly, without energy?

_____

4. What is the advice given at the end of the poem? _____

_____

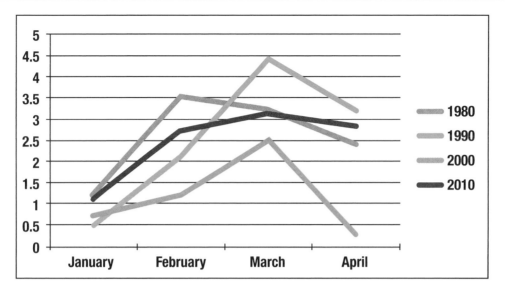

Precipitation (in inches) in Big City

1. In which month and year was precipitation the highest? _____

2. In which month and year was precipitation the lowest? _____

3. How much precipitation fell in February of 1980? _____

4. How much precipitation fell in March of 2000? _____

Oceania

Some geographers label Oceania as a continent. If so, it is the smallest continent by size and the second smallest in terms of population. Oceania is located to the southeast of Asia. It is made up of Australia and a number of island countries. Oceania and its islands are surrounded by the Indian Ocean and the Pacific Ocean.

Much of Oceania's land mass is desert, but there are also very rich and fertile areas. Oceania has some very unique animal life for such a small continent, such as the Koala Bear (which is not really a bear, but a marsupial), the platypus, and the Kangaroo.

Much of Oceania is sparsely populated and there are more sheep in Oceania than people. Oceania is located in the southern hemisphere. This means that its winter is during June, July, and August and its summer during the months of December, January, and February.

Australia was first settled by Europeans as a penal colony or prison colony. The name Australia means "land of the south." There are less people that live in Australia than in the US state of Texas.

1. Most of Oceania is what kind of land? _____ .

2. What is the country that was originally settled as a prison colony? _____

Strength Go to www.summerfitlearning.com for more Activities!

DAILY EXERCISE
Push-ups (traditional or modified)
"Stretch Before You Play!"

Instruction
Repeat 10 times

Be Healthy!
Proteins build and replace tissues in your body.

Colons

A colon really does only one thing: it introduces. It can introduce just about anything: a word, a phrase, a sentence, or a list. Here are some examples.

> Veronica has only one thing on her mind: school.

> Veronica has only one thing on her mind: her math grade.

> Veronica has only one thing on her mind: she wants to pass math.

> Veronica has three things on her mind: fractions, percents, and decimals.

If you aren't sure whether you need a colon in a particular sentence, here is a handy test: read the sentence, and when you reach the colon, substitute the word namely; if the sentence reads through smoothly, then there's a good chance that you do need a colon.

Place the colon correctly in each sentence.

1. I have been to several states Indiana, Utah, California, and Florida.

2. Damion had to decide about the dance should he go or not?

3. There is one place I feel total love and acceptance Grandma's house!

4. Don't forget Mrs. Frank's number one rule read instructions carefully.

5. There were four girls on the committee Brooke, Shelby, Mera, and Barbara.

6. Owen, Stewart and Sam are here were we going somewhere together?

7. Colleen studied very hard for the test English is a tough subject for her.

8. Zachary meant to call one person Evan.

9. Glen doesn't feel well he has a headache and an upset stomach.

10. Curtis has lots of friends he is so easy to get along with.

WEEK 7

Two angles are Adjacent if they have a common side and a common vertex (corner point) and don't overlap.

Angle ABC is adjacent to angle CBD.   Draw a pair of adjacent angles.

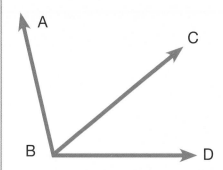

————————————   ————————————

Sedimentary Rock

Over time, rocks are worn away due to erosion. Most of the broken bits of rock end up in streams and rivers that flow down from mountains. These little bits of rock and sand are called sediment. When water slows down (like at a bend in a river), the sediments settle to the bottom. Over many years, layers of rocks settle at the bottom of lakes and oceans. Over time, the layers of sand and mud turn into rocks – sedimentary rocks. There are 6 main kinds:

• **Sandstone** is a soft stone made when sand grains cement together.
• **Shale** is a clay that has been hardened and turned into rock.
• **Limestone** is a rock that may have fossils and is made of calcium carbonate and microscopic shells.
• **Gypsum** is a salt, found where seawater leaves the salt as the water evaporates.
• **Conglomerate** rock has rounded rocks cemented together.
• **Breccia** has jagged bits of rock cemented together. Coal and ironstone are also considered sedimentary rock.

Bake your own sedimentary "rock."

You need ½ cup butter,
1 ½ cups vanilla wafer crumbs
a 14 oz. can of sweetened condensed milk
a 6 oz. package of chocolate chips
a 6 oz. package of peanut butter chips
and 1 cup chopped nuts.

Melt the butter in a clear 13" by 9" baking pan. Sprinkle crumbs over the butter. Pour the condensed milk evenly over the crumbs. Layer the remaining ingredients evenly in the pan. Press down gently. Bake at 350° for 25 to 30 minutes. Cool, then cut into bars. Notice that after being pressed and cooked, your "sedimentary rock" remained in layers!!

Aerobic

Go to www.summerfitlearning.com for more Activities!

DAILY EXERCISE
Moguls
"Stretch Before You Play!"

Instruction
Perform 3 x's for 30 seconds

Be Healthy!
Practice always makes you better.

1

DAY 3

5

WEEK 7

Resolution

The resolution of a story comes at the end. It is when loose ends are tied up and the story ends. It is also called the Falling Action. In this section of the story, everything is explained and tied together.

Read this summary of *A Retrieved Reformation* by O. Henry. Underline the section which is the resolution.

As the story begins, Jimmy Valentine is called to the warden's office. The warden hands Jimmy his pardon from the governor and advises him to stay out of trouble – to stop breaking into safes.

Jimmy leaves prison and meets up with Mike Dolan, a friend and confederate. Jimmy returns to his room above Mike's restaurant where he had lived before detective Ben Price arrested him. Jimmy finds his safe cracking tools still hidden in the wall where he had left them. A week later, a string of bank safe burglaries in the Midwest comes to Ben Price's attention; he knows Jimmy Valentine is back in business and sets out to catch him again. Jimmy arrives in small, remote Elmore, Arkansas, where he plans to rob the bank. Walking toward the hotel, he encounters a beautiful young woman. Their eyes meet, and in that instant, Jimmy undergoes a complete reformation. Jimmy learns she is Annabel Adams, whose father owns the bank. Jimmy continues on to the hotel, where he registers as "Ralph D. Spencer." In a conversation with the hotel clerk, Jimmy learns that Elmore does not have a shoe store and that business is good in the town. Jimmy Valentine does not rob the bank; instead, "Ralph Spencer" settles in Elmore and opens a profitable shoe store.

A year elapses. Jimmy's business is growing, he and Annabel are soon to be married, and Annabel's family has completely accepted him. To cut the ties with his past, Jimmy asks one of his former friends to meet him in Little Rock. Jimmy plans to give the man his set of safe cracking tools. The day before Jimmy is to leave for Little Rock, Ben Price arrives in Elmore, spots Jimmy Valentine, and learns he is about to marry the banker's daughter. Ben Price plans to stop him. The next day before leaving town, with his burglar tools in his suitcase, Jimmy goes to the bank with Annabel, Annabel's sister, and the sister's two little girls, May and Agatha. Annabel's father wants to show off the new burglarproof safe he has recently installed. Ben Price comes into the bank and watches the scene; he tells a bank teller "he is just waiting for a man he knew." Agatha is accidently locked in the safe, which cannot be opened, Mr. Adams exclaims in horror, since the timer and the combination had not been set. Furthermore, Agatha will soon run out of air in the vault. Jimmy and the others can hear Agatha crying out in panic. Annabel turns to Jimmy, begging him to do something, at least to try. Jimmy, knowing he will probably lose Annabel, uses his tools to open the safe in record time, freeing the sobbing child.

Once Agatha is safe, Jimmy puts on his coat and walks away. When he encounters Ben Price, who has witnessed the dramatic scene, Jimmy is ready to turn himself in. But the detective says that he doesn't know Jimmy and walks away. Jimmy is free to stay and work things out.

Why did you choose the sentence(s) which you did? _____

_____

Complimentary angles

Two angles are complimentary if their measures add up to 90.° The angles do not have to be adjacent angles.

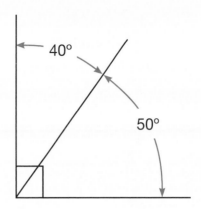

Decide if each of these pairs of angles are complimentary or not. Write **yes** or **no**.

1. 45° and 55° _____

2. 35° and 65° _____

3. 89° and 1° _____

4. 75° and 25° _____

5. 80° and 10° _____

6. 27° and 63° _____

Economy

The United States has a capitalist economy. This is an economic system that encourages private ownership of businesses (such as factories, offices, and shipping enterprises). Supply and demand determine the way in which goods are produced and the means by which income and profit are distributed. Simply put, it is an economic system where anyone can start their own business for their own profit. One of the most basic concepts of economics is that of Supply and Demand. Supply is how much of something is available. If you have 6 pairs of socks, then your supply of socks is 6.

Demand is how much of something people want. If people want 6 pairs of socks, then the demand for socks is 6. Generally speaking, when the demand for something goes up, prices for that something go up as well. This is because the seller thinks people will be willing to pay more money to get what they want. In the same way, price will go down when the demand goes down.

Another term that is helpful to understand is inflation. A simple explanation of inflation is that you can get less for your money than you used to be able to get. You buy a candy bar for 50 cents. A year later, you go to buy the same candy bar and it's 55 cents. You still have only 50 cents, but the price of the candy bar has gone up. The price of that bar has been inflated.

When inflation rises but people's paychecks don't, this means that people have to spend more of their money to buy the same things that they used to be able to buy for less.

1. ___ economy
2. ___ inflation
3. ___ supply
4. ___ demand
5. ___ capitalism

a. you get less for your money than you used to be able to get
b. system that encourages private ownership of businesses
c. how much of something people want
d. the buying and selling of products and services
e. how much of something is available

Strength Go to www.summerfitlearning.com for more Activities!

DAILY EXERCISE
Crunches
"Stretch Before You Play!"

Instruction
Repeat 5 times

Be Healthy!
Not everybody likes sports, and that's okay!

1

2

DAY
4

WEEK 7

Persuasive Paragraph

Persuasive writing allows you to inform and influence others. Speeches, newspaper articles, editorials, advertisements and critical reviews are all forms of persuasive writing. A good persuasive argument should have a strong introduction. It should clearly state the issue and the writer's position. Reasons which support your opinion should be presented logically. The writer should anticipate opposing viewpoints and answer those issues. Finally, you should finish with a strong argument, a summary, or a call to action. In the space below, write a persuasive paragraph defending what you think is the best type of party to attend.

_____

_____

_____

_____

_____

_____

_____

_____

_____

_____

_____

_____

_____

_____

RESPECT – Dalai Lama

The Dalai Lama has said that his life is guided by three major commitments: "the promotion of basic human values such as compassion, forgiveness, tolerance, contentment and self-discipline," the building of harmony among religions, and the welfare of the Tibetan people. The Tibetan people are in a struggle for justice with the Chinese government. The Dalai Lama is hoping to help remove the negative influences of China and restore Tibet's natural environment.

The Dalai Lama was awarded the Nobel Peace Prize in 1989 for his continued non-violent struggle for the freedom of Tibet. He travels the world, speaking to people of all countries. His message of peace and tolerance reflects his respect for all people. He has said, "All major world religions have the same potential to create better human beings. It is therefore important for all religious traditions to respect one another and recognize the value of each other's respective traditions."

1. The Dalai Lama's first commitment is to promote what basic human values?

_____

_____

_____

_____

2. What does harmony mean? _____

_____

_____

3. Why do the Tibetan people need help? _____

_____

_____

4. What does the Dalai Lama feel that religious traditions need to do? _____

_____

_____

Color a star for each time you show Respect through your own actions this week.

 Write a 50-75 word essay describing one of your Respect actions this week.

Respect – Memorize Your Value

"We were taught to respect everyone, especially those who were older and wiser than we were from whom we could learn."

–BeNeca Ward

Core Value Booklist
Read More About Respect

Apples and the Arrow
By Mary and Conrad Buff

A Day's Work
By Eve Bunting

Andy and the Lion
By James Daugherty

········· **TECH TIME!** ·········

Watching and creating animation can be fun. Many web 2.0 tools are available that will let you make this type of creation without any previous experience! Find a tool you like at Summer Fit or through a search and create a brief animation about the ideas of respect that you have learned about this week. Make sure to share your animation with someone, and enjoy the fun together!

www.SummerFitLearning.com

Bill Gates
Tech Guru and Philanthropist
gatesfoundation.org

Play Time!

Choose a Game or Activity to Play for 60 minutes today!

YOU CHOOSE

_____
Write down which game or activity you played today!

 Be Healthy!
Clean the kitchen without being asked.

PARENT TIPS FOR WEEK 8

Skills of the Week

✔ Squares and square roots
✔ Magellan
✔ Analogy
✔ Passive and Active verbs
✔ Irrational numbers
✔ Greenhouse effect
✔ Point of view
✔ New England Colonies
✔ Punctuating items in a series
✔ Cube roots
✔ Genetics
✔ Past participle
✔ Scientific Notation
✔ Hibernation/Dormancy

Weekly Value Responsibility

Rachel Carson

Being responsible means others can depend on you. It is being accountable for what you do and for what you do not do.

A lot of times it is easier to look to someone else to step forward and do the work or to blame others when it does not get done. You are smart, capable and able so try to be the person who accepts challenges and does not blame others if it does not get done.

GET FIT TIME!

Stretching is Very Important
Get into the habit of stretching every night before you go to bed, as well as before you exercise every day.

Play 60 Every Day!
Run, jump, dance and have fun outside every day for 60 minutes!

Health and Wellness

Have a passion! Get excited about something and commit yourself to it. Do it often, whether it is a sport or activity – but always do it safely!

WEEK 8

Check the ☑ As You Complete Your Daily Task

	Day 1	Day 2	Day 3	Day 4	Day 5
MIND	☐	☐	☐	☐	☐
BODY	☐	☐	☐	☐	☐
DAILY READING	☐	☐	☐	☐	☐
	30 minutes	30 minutes	30 minutes	30 minutes	30 minutes

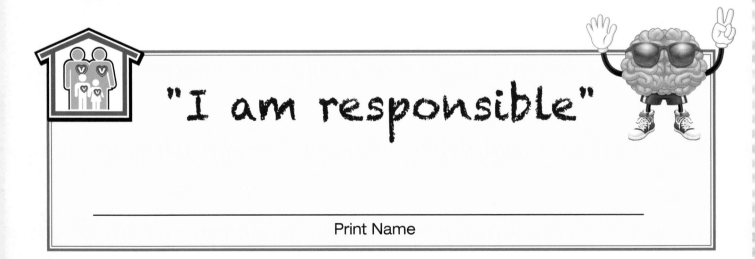

"I am responsible"

_____
Print Name

A square number is the number you get when you multiply a number by itself. 5 squared (5^2) = 5 x 5 or 25. Finding a square root is the inverse of squaring a number. In other words, the square root of 25 is the number that multiplied by itself will give the product 25.

Square each of the following numbers.

1. 2 _____
2. 7 _____
3. 6 _____

4. 8 _____
5. 3 _____
6. 9 _____

Find the square root of the following numbers.

7. 25 _____
8. 36 _____

9 81 _____
10. 9 _____

Analogy

An analogy is a comparison between two different things in order to highlight some point of similarity. It works much like a simile or metaphor, the difference being that the analogy focuses on being similar – not being the same.

For example: Children are like flowers in a garden. Each one is different, and that difference adds to the beauty of the group. Some flourish with lots of attention, others do better when left alone once in awhile. They have basic needs – food, shelter, and love rather than dirt and pruning. They can both bring joy to those around them.

Sometimes an analogy is very simple: Go is to green as stop is to red. This simple phrase compares the colors of the stoplight to the meanings of the colors.

See if you can finish these simple analogies.

1. In is to Out as Up is to _____ .
2. Toe is to Foot as Finger is to _____ .
3. Three is to Triangle as Four is to _____ .
4. Land is to River as Body is to _____ .
5. Panel is to Door as Pane is to _____ .
6. Word is to Sentence as Page is to _____ .
7. Author is to Story as Poet is to _____ .
8. Gas is to Car as Wood is to _____ .
9. Knife is to Cut as Pen is to _____ .
10. Lion is to Cage as Book is to _____ .
11. Fish is to Gills as Human is to _____ .
12. Six legs is to Ant as Eight legs is to _____ .
13. Pencil is to Write as Crayon is to _____ .
14. Sit is to Sat as Bring is to _____ .
15. Cat is to Mouse as Spider is to _____ .

DAILY EXERCISE
Racing Leap-Frog
"Stretch Before You Play!"

Instruction
Play with Friends!

Be Healthy!
Your body is growing and needs 8-9 hours of sleep every day!

DAY 1

WEEK 8

Magellan

Magellan left Spain in 1519 with five ships. It took more than fourteen months to find the southern opening to the Pacific Ocean. He found it in the frigid, stormy waters now known as the Strait of Magellan. What Magellan did not count on was the immensity of the Pacific, a body of water larger than all of the land on earth. Magellan expected Asia to be a few hundred miles beyond the coast of South America. Instead, the expedition traveled 12,600 miles before reaching land. The starving sailors arrived the island of Guam after more than six months at sea, and then moved on to the Philippines. There, Magellan was killed in a battle. Only one of Magellan's five ships made it back to Spain, just twelve days less than three years after their journey started. Only that ship and eighteen sailors remained of the 265 men who accompanied Magellan.

1. What was significant about Magellan's voyage? _____

_____

2. What might have been difficult for the sailors in Magellan's crew? _____

_____

Active Verbs

Active verb refers to the way a verb is used in the sentence. There are action verbs, which are doing words, and there are verbs of being or linking verbs. These are verbs such as am, are, is, was, werte. All of these can be used in active case. In active case, the subject performs the action of the verb.

For each sentence, if the verb is active, write an A, if it is not, write an N.

1. _____ Adele and Adelaide picked berries from the bushes.
2. _____ The salesman urged the Jensens to purchase the new computer.
3. _____ The racecars zipped around the track at tremendous speeds.
4. _____ The Aguillars were surprised by the number of events at the fair.
5. _____ The warehouse stores were filled with all kinds of Christmas bargains.
6. _____ The football team consumed a mountain of food prior to the game.
7. _____ The houses on the road were all painted in similar colors.
8. _____ Birds of many varieties winged their way south for the winter months.
9. _____ The trees reached their beautiful branches toward the lofty clouds.
10. _____ The flowers on the side of the road waved as we passed by.

Irrational numbers

An irrational number is a number that cannot be written as a fraction. A rational number can be written as a fraction or a ratio (hence, rational). 2.5 is rational because it can be written as 5/2. 6 is rational because it can be written as 6/1. 0.25 is rational because it can be written as 1/4. All repeating decimals are rational.

Some numbers are irrational because they cannot be written as a fraction or a ration. The number pi (π) is a well-known irrational number. It is written 3.141592653 and continues. Many people use 22/7 as a fraction to represent pi, but it is not accurate. $\sqrt{2}$ is an irrational number because the square root of two cannot be written as a fraction or ratio. Many square roots and cube roots are irrational numbers.

Are the following numbers rational or irrational?

1. _____ 1.3333333

2. _____ $\sqrt{4}$

3. _____ 16%

4. _____ 0.6

5. _____ $\sqrt{7}$

6. _____ $\pi = 3.141592654$

Greenhouse Effect

The earth has been compared to a greenhouse. The atmosphere (several layers of gases) works like the windows on the greenhouse. Sunlight shines in and warms everything during the day, and since the heat is trapped inside, it stays warm as long as the sun is shining and stays fairly warm at night, too. People talk about the Greenhouse Effect in a negative way. That's because there is concern that too much carbon dioxide and other greenhouse gases in the air are making the greenhouse effect stronger and the earth is getting warmer than it should. Planting more trees would help because trees take in carbon dioxide and give off oxygen. Instead, many forests are being cut down and not replaced. The oceans can absorb some of the carbon dioxide, also, but not nearly enough. The increased carbon dioxide in the ocean changes the water, making it more like acid, which ocean animals don't like. Scientists think global warming could lead to more devastating hurricanes and severe heat waves. We may lose some of the earth's water, which would limit electricity generated through water power. Changes in climate will affect most ecosystems and affect the life cycles of plants and animals. Some habitats may disappear; the animals that need those conditions may die out.

What can you do? Some suggestions are reduce waste, watch your water use, use less energy, walk when possible, or use a bicycle. And spread the word. Talk to others about what you and they can do to help ease this problem.

1. What are two possible effects of global warming?_____

_____

2. What is one thing you could do to help deal with this problem? _____

_____

DAY 2

4

5

WEEK 8

Strength Go to www.summerfitlearning.com for more Activities!

DAILY EXERCISE
Chop n Squat
"Stretch Before You Play!"

Instruction
Repeat 10 times

Be Healthy!
Your brain works hard everyday, so put on a helmet!

DAY
2

Point of View

Point of view is the perspective from which a speaker or writer recounts a narrative or presents information. Depending on the topic, purpose, and audience, writers of nonfiction may rely on the first-person point of view (I, we), the second-person (you, your), or the third-person (he, she, it, they). Most stories are written in First or Third Person. Second Person is used more commonly in instructions.

Determine whether each example below is told in First, Second, or Third Person.

1. _____ The children were running everywhere around the park. We were trying to keep track of the Tate children, whom we were tending, but it was difficult with so many children in one place!

2. _____ The children were running everywhere around the park. They climbed the ladders to the slides, hung from the tree branches, ran through the sandboxes, and ran around the swing sets. They yelled and screamed joyously.

3. _____ Once upon a time there was a king. He lived in a kingdom far away and was very happy there. He thought he had everything he ever needed to stay happy. I am that king, and this is the story of how I found what I truly needed.

4. _____ Making a sandcastle is a favorite project of beach-goers of all ages. Begin by digging up a large amount of sand (enough to fill at least six pails) and arranging it in a pile. Then, scoop the sand into your pail, patting it down and leveling it off at the rim as you do.

5. _____ The sun was high in the sky. The clouds had drifted away. The breezes had blown off to harass someone else. There seemed no movement in the area at all – except for me, as I trudged my lonely way down the seemingly deserted highway.

6. _____ Making a sandcastle is a favorite project of beach-goers of all ages. Margaret was no exception. She was determined to build the best sand castle this particular beach had ever seen.

7. _____ The sun was high in the sky. The clouds had drifted away. The breezes had blown off to harass someone else. There seemed no movement in the area at all – except for Juan, as he trudged his lonely way down the seemingly deserted highway.

8. _____ How do you know what your friends are up to? Can you call them anytime you want? Do they post their activities on a social network site? Do they send you tweets and instant messages? Do you even want to know what they are up to all the time?

Scientific notation is the way that scientists easily handle very large numbers or very small numbers. For example, instead of writing 0.0000000056, we write 5.6×10^{-9}. How does this work? We can think of 5.6×10^{-9} as the product of two numbers: 5.6, the digit term, and 10^{-9}, the exponential term. When we use this method, there is always one number in the one's place. The exponent of 10 is the number of places the decimal point must be shifted to give the number in long form. A positive exponent shows that the decimal point has been shifted that number of places to the right. A negative exponent shows that the decimal point has been shifted that number of places to the left. A negative exponent is used for a number less than 0.

Write each number using scientific notation.

1. 3, 230, 000 _____

2. 1,000, 000, 000 _____

3. 0.00000013 _____

4. 0.0045 _____

Write the following numbers out.

5. 4.56×10^6 _____

6. 2.3×10^4 _____

7. 2.3×10^{-3} _____

8. 7.61×10^{-5} _____

New England Colonies

Most of the people who settled in the New England Colonies wanted to keep their family together and practice their own religion. They were used to doing many things themselves and not depending on other people for much. Some of these people came to New England to make money, but they were not the majority. The New England Colonies were largely farming and fishing communities. Shipbuilding was also an important business, as was the trade that depended on it. This area was well suited to these pursuits, due to the large forests, abundant bays, and natural ports. The people made their own clothes and shoes. They grew much of their own food. Crops like corn and wheat grew in large amounts, and much was shipped to England. Foods that didn't grow in America were shipped from England. Boston was the major New England port. Education was very important to the people of the New England colonies. The parents wanted their children to be able to read the Bible. This shows that religion was very important to the New England colonists as well.

1. Why were forests important for the shipbuilding business? _____

_____

2. Why did the New England colonists think education was important? _____

_____

Aerobic

Go to www.summerfitlearning.com for more Activities!

DAILY EXERCISE
Bear Crawl
"Stretch Before You Play!"

Instruction
Crawl for 2 Minutes x 3

Be Healthy!
Eat a healthy snack like popcorn!

Punctuate items in a series

When you group several names or make a list, you are writing a series of things. To make your meaning clear, you must often separate the items with commas. For example, look at the sentence: **Allison went to the game with Mary Lou George and Sue**. Did Allison go with four people – Mary, Lou, George, and Sue? Did she go with three people – Mary Lou, George and Sue? Or did she go with only two people – a girl named Mary Lou George and a girl named Sue.

If there are only two items, a comma is not needed, but if there are three or more, you need those commas. **In the sentences below, place commas.**

1. Kendra Sandra and Peter were leaving for the movie.
2. Keisha and Samantha were feeding their puppy cat and bird.
3. I'm doing a food and drink experiment to discover which snacks are delicious nutritious colorful and fun.
4. The train runs to Indianapolis Lafayette and Chicago.
5. Mother read a story which had a surprising unusual vivid and thoroughly enchanting ending.
6. We bought potatoes onions carrots and spices to add to the stew.
7. There was a strong wind the temperature had dropped and it was raining.
8. She packed a purple skirt a pair of black slacks and her best shoes for the trip.

Hibernation / dormancy

During the colder months of the year, humans tend to stay inside more, or if they are outside, they dress warmer. Some animals migrate from an area with colder climate to a warmer area, but some animals do not migrate. These are mainly animals with an ability to reduce their needs and go into a suspended animation sort of state – they hibernate. This resembles a deep sleep, but it is more than that. The body functions literally slow down and body temperature drops. Animals that hibernate must first build up body fat reserves, storing energy that can fuel the body while they sleep. Some animals hibernate for several months, like bears. Others, like chipmunks, may be dormant (inactive) for a short time, then awaken and "snack," then go back to dormancy.

1. How do humans compensate for the lower temperatures of the winter seasons? ______

____

2. What happens during hibernation? ______________________

____

3. Why do hibernating animals build up body fat reserves? ______________

____

A cubed number is the number you get when you multiply a number by itself, and then multiply it by itself again. This is not the same as multiplying a number by 3.

5 cubed (5³) = 5 x 5 x 5 or 125.

The cube root is the number that multiplied by itself and by itself again will give the desired product. **Tell the cube of the following numbers.**

1. 3 _____

2. 1.5 _____

3. 5 _____

4. 8 _____

5. 3.2 _____

6. 9 _____

Tell the cube root of each of the following.

7. 27 _____

8. 8 _____

Genetics

Inside every cell of each living thing are sets of instructions called genes. The genes provide the instructions on what is the plant or animal, what it looks like, how it is to survive, and how it will interact with its surrounding environment. The genes are strung together in long stands of material called deoxyribonucleic acid (DNA) and these long strands are called chromosomes. Most living things have pairs of chromosomes (one from each parent), though they may have a different number of chromosomes from another living thing. For example, humans have 23 pairs of chromosomes and the fruit fly has 4 pairs.

Each person has two genes for eye color. When a person has two identical genes, he will have eyes of that color. Another person may have two different genes, and she will have eyes the color of the dominant gene. With eye color, the gene for brown eyes is dominant (B). The gene for blue eyes is recessive (b). If a person has one B gene and one b gene or two B genes, then that person will have brown eyes. If a person has bb eye genes, then the person will have blue eyes. Green and hazel eyes have to do with the pigment melanin which is found in eyes, so the simple explanation above is really part of a more complex total process.

1. Most living things have how many chromosomes from each parent? _____

_____

2. How many more pairs of chromosomes do humans have than fruit flies? _____

_____

3. Which eye color gene is dominant in humans? _____

4. What two genes does a person have to have to possess blue eyes? _____

_____

DAILY EXERCISE	Instruction
Side Step	**Repeat 5 times in**
"Stretch Before You Play!"	**each direction**

Be Healthy!
Smile!

Passive verbs

With an active verb, the subject performs the action of the verb. With a passive verb, the action is performed on the subject. Consider the following sentences:

Hal fed the two cats.

The two cats were fed by Hal.

In the first sentence, the action is performed by the subject; in the second sentence the action is performed on the subject. **In the following sentences, mark A for Active and P for Passive. If the sentence uses an active verb, change it to passive.**

1. _____ The flowers were watered by different members of the class. _____
_____

2. _____ The cows placidly ate the grass in the meadow. _____
_____

3. _____ The litter along the highway was being cleaned up by the boy scout troop._____
_____

4. _____ The truck pulling the boat passed the semi on the freeway._____
_____

5. _____ The scenery for the play had been painted by the technical crew. _____
_____

Past Participle

One of the most common problems with verbs is knowing when to use the past form and when to use the past participle form with irregular verbs. The past participle requires a helping verb, such as am, is, are, has, have. We might say, "I seen that movie", but that would be incorrect. Seen is the past participle form and needs a helping verb. A correct statement would be "I have seen that movie."

For the sentences below, underline the correct verb form from the choices given.

1. I should have (knew , known) that Janson would be late.
2. You could have (froze , frozen) your toes by getting your feet wet in that cold.
3. He (began , begun) his talk with a little joke.
4. My brand new coat was (stole , stolen) from the hallway.
5. I really liked that dress, but it was (tore , torn).
6. The police (knew , known) who stole the money.
7. Babbette sang the song that was (chose , chosen) by the committee.
8. The telephone (rang , rung) just as I started to study.
9. The book I would have (chose , chosen) was not on the shelf.
10. Our doorbell is (wore , worn) out because it is so old.

WEEK 8

RRESPONSIBILITY – Rachel Carson

Rachel Carson believed that we must demonstrate responsibility for the preservation of our planet. She loved nature, studying marine biology and zoology in college. She wrote about conservation and natural resources. Her first three books focused on the seas and the oceans and their wonders.

After World War II, Rachel became aware of the dangers of the use of pesticides in agriculture. In her book *Silent Spring*, she chastised the government and agricultural scientists for the negative long-term effects of pesticides. She called for a change in the way people view the natural world. She urged people to be more responsible in their use of resources. She testified before congress to request new policies to protect human health and the environment. She was a pioneer in the movement to care for our environment so that it will be strong and vibrant.

RESPONSIBILITY

1. What are pesticides? _____

2. Unscramble the following words from the story. _____

   ascnntoivreo _____

   lagcurritula _____

   scroseeru _____

   brelisnotipsyi _____

3. What are some ways you can use resources responsibly?_____

   _____

   _____

   _____

Color a star for each time you show Responsibility through your own actions this week.

 Write a 50-75 word essay describing one of your Responsibility actions this week.

Responsibility Memorize Your Value

"The price of greatness is responsibility."

– Sir Winston Churchill

Core Value Booklist
Read More About Responsibiliby

Uncommon Champions: Fifteen Athletes Who Battled Back
By Mary Kaminsky

The Value of Responsibility: The Story of Ralph Bunche
By Ann Donegan Johnson

Following Isabella
By Linda Talley and Andrea Chase

·········TECH TIME!·········

There are many things to be responsible for throughout your life. Reflect on the responsibilities involved with the information you learned on risks of bio-hazards. What is your responsibility to the environment? Are you being as responsible as you can for your environment? Take some time to measure your Carbon Footprint. You can take a survey online (answer as best you can) and get an idea of ways you are affecting the area around you based on the responsible decisions you make daily. Show your parents your rating and discuss how your family can improve it. Let us know your Carbon Footprint too!

www.SummerFitLearning.com

Bill Gates
Tech Guru and Philanthropist
gatesfoundation.org

Play Time!

Choose a Game or Activity to Play for 60 minutes today!

YOU CHOOSE

_____

Write down which game or activity you played today!

Be Healthy!
Drink water instead of soda.

PARENT TIPS FOR WEEK 9

Skills of the Week

✔ Simple equations, linear equations
✔ Context
✔ Latin words
✔ Southern colonies
✔ Redundancy
✔ Graphing linear equations
✔ Animal migration
✔ Triangles
✔ Magna Carta
✔ Palindromes
✔ Irony
✔ Ellipses

Weekly Value Perseverance

Sally Ride

Perseverance means not giving up or giving in when things are difficult. It means you try again when you fail.

Sometimes it is easy to forget that a lot of things in life require patience and hard work. Do not give up because it is hard to accomplish a task or to get something that we want. Focus on your goal and keep working hard. It is through this experience that you will accomplish what you want.

Stretching is Very Important

Get into the habit of stretching every night before you go to bed, as well as before you exercise every day.

Play 60 Every Day!

Run, jump, dance and have fun outside every day for 60 minutes!

Health and Wellness

You don't have to "diet" to be at a healthy weight. Eat different types of foods, including different vegetables and fruits, and stay away from the soda machine! Being involved in a sport or playing and getting physical activity everyday keeps you at a healthy weight, too!

WEEK 9

Check the ☑ As You Complete Your Daily Task

	Day 1	Day 2	Day 3	Day 4	Day 5
MIND	☐	☐	☐	☐	☐
BODY	☐	☐	☐	☐	☐
DAILY READING	☐ 30 minutes	☐ 30 minutes	☐ 30 minutes	☐ 30 minutes	☐ 30 minutes

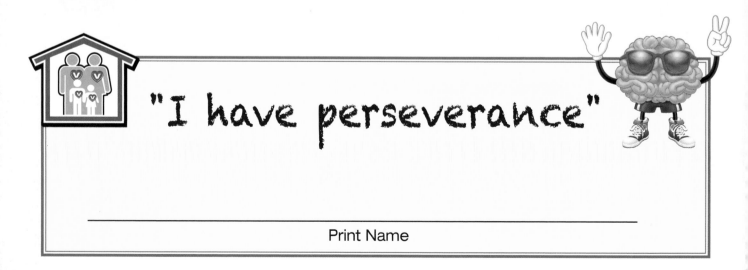

"I have perseverance"

_____
Print Name

Practice solving simple equations

1. $7x + 5 = -51$

2. $5x + 7x = 72$

3. $4x - 6 = 6x$

4. $3x - 8 = 22$

5. $3x - 1 = 34 - 4x$

6. $3 + 4x - 2 = 4x + 4 - x$

7. $24 - 3x + 5 = 9x - 7$

8. $4x + 9 + x = 6 + 3x + 1$

9. $2x + 11 - 1x = 4x + 2 - 2x$

10. $3x \times 8 = 72 - 2x + 6$

Ellipses

What are ellipses? They are the three little dots you sometimes see in a story or other piece of writing. The most common usage is to show the reader that some words have been left out, perhaps from a quotation or an excerpt of a story.

Here's a quote from the book *Our Mutual Friend* by Charles Dickens: "I cannot help it; reason has nothing to do with it; I love her against reason." If I wanted to make a point about the focus of the quote, I'd be tempted to shorten it to this: "I cannot help it . . . I love her against reason." The middle part—"reason has nothing to do with it"—seems redundant, and taking it out doesn't change the meaning. Ellipses can also be used to show a pause in the flow of a sentence, or quoted speech: Julia wondered and wondered ... and continued to wonder for a very long time.

Decide what phrase in each of the selections below could be replace by ellipses. Underline the phrase.

1. The story is about children who live on Mars and have never seen the sun. One girl has seen the sun, however, and the other children are jealous. She describes the sun to them in great detail. The children decide to lock the girl in the closet to "punish" her for telling them about the sun.

2. When making popcorn in the microwave, you simply have to follow the instructions on the package. Sometimes the instructions are on the front and sometimes they are on the back. If you follow them carefully, you should get a full bag of the tasty treat.

Aerobic

DAILY EXERCISE
Towel Slide/Plate Push
"Stretch Before You Play!"

Instruction
Complete 5 times

Be Healthy!
Brush your teeth in the morning, afternoon and before bed.

DAY 1

WEEK 9

3 4 5

Context

   Context can be used in a couple of ways in literature. You can use the conditions and circumstances that are relevant to an event or fact. If a person walks out of the bowling alley and complains loudly about the atmosphere and the condition of the lanes, you could use that information to infer that the person had not bowled well. Context can also help with word meaning. In this case, context consists of the parts of a piece of writing, speech, etc., that precede and follow a word or passage and contribute to its full meaning. If you have the sentence: **A sleuth, such as Sherlock Holmes, can be very helpful in solving crimes**, you can deduce that the word sleuth means a detective.

Use the context of the following sentences to help you determine the meaning of the underlined words.

1. The emergency room doctors see patients with <u>trauma</u>, such as a broken bone, every night.
_____

2. In the fall, the bright <u>foliage</u> is a delight to see. Red, orange, and yellow leaves and vegetation paint the world for our enjoyment. _____
_____

3. We could tell by the rotten smell, that something <u>putrid</u> was in our trash can.
_____

4. Grandpa didn't know that Suzie was coming along on the fishing trip, and now he had to <u>alter</u> his plans. _____
_____

5. The children were <u>perched</u> on the edge of the sofa arms, waiting to hop off and land on the next unlucky passerby. _____
_____

6. With the field torn up by the players' cleats, and the cold rain falling in waves, conditions on the playing field were <u>dismal</u>. _____
_____

7. Jeremiah joked around so much that when he told the others about the accident that had occurred, they didn't believe that he was being <u>earnest</u>. _____
_____

8. Jake asked his mother for permission to go to his friend Rodney's dance party, stating that his grades had improved, and he was quite pleased when she <u>consented</u>.
_____

Solve simple linear equations

A linear equation is an equation for a straight line. They usually have two variables, an x and a y. The easiest way to solve a linear equation is to make a table with two columns. The left hand column represents the x variable and the right hand column represents the y variable. You choose several numbers to go one column and solve for the other number.

Example: $y = 2x + 1$

x	y
1	3
2	5
3	7

The ordered pairs would be (1, 3), (2, 5) and (3, 7)

Using 1, 2, and 3 for x, find three ordered pairs for each equation.

1. $y = 2x + 6$	
2. $2x - y = -5$	
3. $4x - 4y = 8$	

Southern Colonies

The founders of the Southern Colonies brought their families, as did the New England colonists, and they kept their families together on the plantations. Their main motivation was to make the good money that was available in the new American market.

The Southern Colonies were almost entirely agricultural. The warm climate made it possible to grow crops throughout the year and was well suited for plantations. A plantation was a large plot of land that contained a great many acres of farmland and buildings. A large part of the workforce was African slaves, who first arrived in 1619. Some of the Southern plantations were very complex and consisted of the main house, slave quarters, a dairy, blacksmith's shop, laundry, smokehouse and barns which made the plantations to large degree, self-sufficient. Crops were traded for items that could not be produced on the plantations including farm tools, shoes, lace, and dishes. Southern planters grew tobacco, rice, and indigo, which they sold to buyers in England and elsewhere in America.

1. What were some of the buildings other than houses found on plantations? _____

_____

2. What were some of the items which could not be produced on the plantation? _____

_____

DAY 2

4

5

WEEK 9

DAILY EXERCISE
Balance
"Stretch Before You Play!"

Instruction
Hold each for 15 seconds, then switch legs and repeat

Be Healthy!
Turn off the TV and play outside.

DAY 2

WEEK 9

Redundancy

Synonyms for redundant include superfluous, unnecessary, needless, excessive, spare, or repetitive. In speaking, we say something is redundant if it repeats something that has already been said. Sometimes we are redundant intentionally, such as when we want to emphasize a point. Frequently we are simply falling into common expressions without thinking. For example, we may speak of a "free gift." If it's a gift, of course it's free. **In the following sentences, cross out one of the words that makes the sentence redundant.**

1. The general decided to advance the troops forward to win the battle.
2. The tern plunged down into the water to grab the fish.
3. The underground subway was full of people going to the city.
4. He composed a truly sincere letter of apology.
5. Teddy told the exact same story to his parents as Rusty told to his parents.
6. Steven tended to over exaggerate his stories.
7. In the front of the book was a beautifully illustrated drawing.
8. The store specialized in foreign imports.
9. Cameron sustained several harmful injuries in the accident.
10. The professors may possibly meet to discuss the problems the students are having.

Vocabulary – Latin roots

A root, as its name suggests, is a word or word part from which other words grow, usually through the addition of prefixes and suffixes. The root of the word vocabulary, for example, is voc, a Latin root meaning "word" or "name." This root also appears in the words advocacy, convocation, evocative, vocal, and vociferous. Understanding the meanings of the common word roots can help us deduce the meanings of new words that we encounter. **Use the meanings of these roots to match the vocabulary word with the correct definition.**

Dict, dic, dit – speak, declare	Vent, ven – to come
1. ___ Advent	a. A decree issued by a sovereign or other authority; any authoritative command
2. ___ Covenant	b. A speaking evil of or to a person; an imprecation; curse
3. ___ Edict	c. To give up or renounce (duties or high office, etc.) in a public, voluntary or formal manner
4. ___ Intervene	d. An arrival; a start or commencement; the coming of Christ into the world
5. ___ Malediction	e. To come between disputing people or groups; to intercede or mediate
6. ___ Circumvent	f. A formal agreement of legal validity; a conditional pledge or promise
7. ___ Abdicate	g. To go around or bypass; to avoid by artfulness; to elude

Using the equation y = 2x + 3, find 3 ordered pairs for the equation. Plot those pairs on the line graph and draw the line – the linear equation!

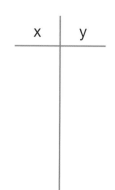

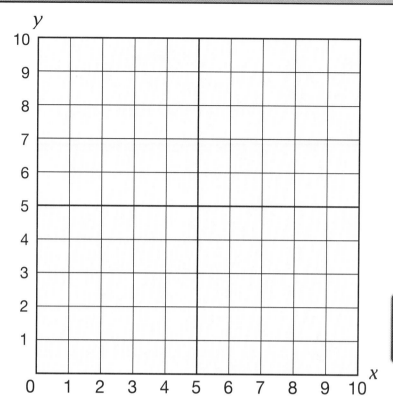

Animal Migration

Many animals migrate, traveling to avoid bad weather, to find food, or to reproduce. Some migrators travel short distances, other go thousands of miles. Migrators travel by flying, swimming, walking, hopping, burrowing, or slithering. True migrators make a two-way trip each year from one place to another and back again. Migrating animals usually use the same routes year after year. The movement of migratory animals usually corresponds with seasonal changes. Many animals migrate to northern regions during summer months. The long summer days in the northernmost portions of the world ensure a good food supply. As fall and colder weather approaches, many animals migrate south to find warm winter weather and available food. Many scientists view animal migration as an adaptation. Animals that have learned to move to optimal environments are the ones who have survived to continue their species. Humans travel, too, and sometimes with regularity. Many people take a yearly vacation.

Use the chart below to think about the differences between yearly trips by humans and animals.

Humans	Animals
Use a map to find a place	
Go for enjoyment and relaxation	
Travel with family	
Gasoline is usually needed for fuel	
Create a habitat wherever they go	

Aerobic

Go to www.summerfitlearning.com for more Activities!

DAILY EXERCISE
Jump Rope
"Stretch Before You Play!"

Instruction
**Goal = 5 minutes
without stopping**

Be Healthy!
Slow down
when you eat!

Palindrome

A palindrome is a word or phrase which reads the same in both directions. Some simple examples are: racecar, level, civic, madam and radar. An example of a palindrome phase is: **Step on no pets**. These are character-by-character palindromes.

Another type of palindrome is the word-unit palindrome. In this type, the words form the same sentence in either directions: **Women understand men, few men understand women.**

Circle the words in each sentence which are palindromes.

1. Timothy asked Hannah for some books.

2. Sheila gave the bookmarks to Coco and Anna.

3. The political rally was being held at the Civic Center.

4. The concert featured some duets and some solos.

5. The boys took the kayak down the river.

6. Did you have to refer to your notes during the speech?

7. They had pizza with carrots and a pepper, Madam.

8. The officer caught the speeder on his radar.

9. We need to repaper the walls.

10. The ancient Viking sagas were interesting stories.

Decide if each of the following sentences or phrases is a palindrome (yes or no).

11. _____ Cigar? Toss it in a can. It is so tragic.

12. _____ A man, a plan, a canal: Panama Canal.

13. _____ Rise to vote, sir.

14. _____ Too bad I hid a boot.

15. _____ Won't I panic in a pit, Eve?

Can you prove that the measures of the three angles of a triangle add up to 180°? Sure you can. Draw a triangle on a regular piece of paper – it can be any size, but should take up most of the paper. Then cut the angles apart (figure a). Next lay the three angles next to each other (figure b). Since they form a straight line, the total measure is 180.° If you want to be sure, try this with a couple of different shaped and different size triangles.

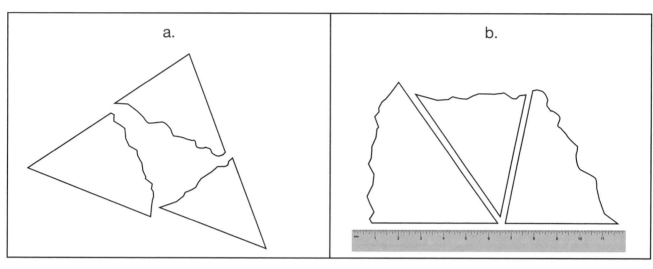

a.

b.

Magna Carta

By the 1000s, the kings of England had been getting pretty powerful. That was fine as long as the kings were good kings, like William the Conqueror or Henry II. When King Richard died in 1199, his younger brother John became king, and John was not such a good king.

First he lost almost all of the English land to France. Then he made everyone who owned land in England pay extra taxes. He got into disagreements with the Pope about who would control the Catholic Church in England. King John's fight with the Pope got so bad that the Pope excommunicated him, although they later worked out their differences.

The wealthy men of England - the earls, the dukes, and the counts - decided to try to get back some of the power from the king. They wrote a letter (Latin "carta") saying that everyone in England would have certain rights that the king could not take away from them anymore.

The Magna Carta stressed that even the king had to obey the law. He also had to make sure people knew the laws – he couldn't just make up a new law on the spur of the moment. Many people consider this the beginning of democratic government. The people (through the nobles) changed how they were treated – for the better.

1. Should the nobles have forced this law upon the king? Explain _____

_____

_____

_____

_____

_____

DAILY EXERCISE
Toe Taps
"Stretch Before You Play!"

Instruction
**Repeat 10 times
with each foot**

Be Healthy!
Walk with your
family before
or after dinner.

Irony

Irony is a contrast between what is expected and what actually exists or happens. For example, when a criminal robs a police station that would be considered ironic. Another example is the person who slipped in a mud puddle on her way out of the cleaners.

Decide whether each of the following is an example of irony or not (yes or no).

1. _____ The traffic cop had 20 unpaid parking tickets.

2. _____ The traffic cop gave 20 parking tickets.

3. _____ A person with a sign saying, "Get a brain" spells the next word wrong.

4. _____ A person with a sign saying, "Get a brain" gets arrested.

5. _____ The security guard is awake and alert.

6. _____ The security guard is asleep behind his desk.

7. _____ "15 best things about our public schools" was seen on a billboard.

8. _____ A person was standing by a no smoking sign to smoke a cigarette.

9. _____ The boy was crossing a crosswalk correctly.

10. _____ A crossing guard was crossing against the light.

11. _____ I saw a sign that says "Fish of the Day – Halibut".

12. _____ I saw a sign that says "Fish of the Day – Roast Beef".

13. _____ Your parents finally let you have a kitten, and you are allergic to cats.

14. _____ Susan doesn't like Mary, but she wants to buy the same outfit Mary has.

15. _____ You've studied for the spelling test, but spell your own name wrong.

16. _____ You've studied for the spelling test and get 100%.

17. _____ You get great candy on Halloween and eat it all.

18. _____ You get great candy on Halloween and get braces the next day.

WEEK 9

DAY 4

1 2 3 4 5

PERSEVERANCE – Sally Ride

Sally Ride was the first woman in space. This in itself was a great feat. In 1979, she completed a one-year training and evaluation period, and was assigned as a Mission Specialist on future space shuttle flight crews. She performed as an on-orbit Capsule Communicator on the STS-2 and STS-3 missions, and participated in several other missions for NASA.

However, Ride did not stop trying to achieve or rest on her previous achievements. She continued to work to broaden the minds of others in scientific fields. She became a professor of physics at the University of California San Diego and the Director of the University of California's California Space Institute. She founded her own company, Sally Ride Science, with the intention of motivating girls and young women to science, math and technology based careers. She wrote five books for children. She also helped direct education projects to help interest middle school students in areas of science.

Ride continued to persevere in encouraging others, especially young women, to study and work in scientific fields. Her final battle was with cancer, which she fought for 17 months, before dying in the summer of 2012.

1. Sally Ride was the first woman to do what?_____

2. Ride wanted to encourage young women to careers in what three areas? _____

_____

3. What does the word previous mean? _____

4. Explain how Sally Ride demonstrated perseverance. _____

_____

_____

5. What is one of your big goals in life? _____

_____

Color a star for each time you show
Perseverance through your own actions this week.

Write a 50-75 word essay describing one of your Perseverance actions this week.

Perseverance – Memorize Your Value

"It always seems impossible until its done."

– Nelson Mandela

Core Value Booklist
Read More About Perseverance

Fly, Eagle, Fly
By Desmond Tuto

I Knew You Could
By Wally Piper

Strawberry Girl
By Lois Lenski

·········TECH TIME!·········

To persevere in something is not always easy. Many people find that it is easier to do this when you can be organized. If you can keep yourself organized, you can see your goals, meet them, and perhaps go beyond them. Web 2.0 tools that help keep you organized are helpful because they are available anywhere you can access the Internet. Try out an organization tool linked on our site or one you find on your own. Focus on the perseverance of Sally Ride. Create an online binder or portfolio with at least 3 pages (links to websites) about her!

www.SummerFitLearning.com

Bill Gates
Tech Guru and
Philanthropist
gatesfoundation.org

Play Time!

Choose a Game or Activity to Play for 60 minutes today!

YOU CHOOSE

_____

Write down which game or activity you played today!

Be Healthy!
Acne, also known as pimples, is a normal part of growing up.

DAY 5

WEEK 9

PARENT TIPS FOR WEEK 10

Skills of the Week

✔ Angle measurement
✔ Boston Massacre
✔ Cause and effect
✔ Apostrophe
✔ Mean, median, mode, range
✔ Boiling and melting points
✔ Vocabulary
✔ Probability
✔ Lexington and Concord
✔ Volume
✔ Precipitates
✔ Suffixes
✔ Homophones

Weekly Value Friendship

Friendship is what comes from being friends. It is caring and sharing and being there for each other in good times and bad.

J.R.R. Tolkien and C. S. Lewis

It is fun to have friends that we play with, go to the movies and share our time, but it also is a responsibility. Our friends are people that we trust, protect, respect and stand up for even when it is not easy. We care about our friends and our friends care about us.

Stretching is Very Important
Get into the habit of stretching every night before you go to bed, as well as before you exercise every day.

Play 60 Every Day!

Run, jump, dance and have fun outside every day for 60 minutes!

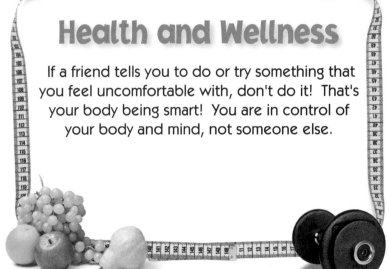

Health and Wellness

If a friend tells you to do or try something that you feel uncomfortable with, don't do it! That's your body being smart! You are in control of your body and mind, not someone else.

WEEK 10

HEALTHY MIND + HEALTHY BODY

Check the ✓ As You Complete Your Daily Task

	Day 1	Day 2	Day 3	Day 4	Day 5
MIND	☐	☐	☐	☐	☐
BODY	☐	☐	☐	☐	☐
DAILY READING	☐ 30 minutes	☐ 30 minutes	☐ 30 minutes	☐ 30 minutes	☐ 30 minutes

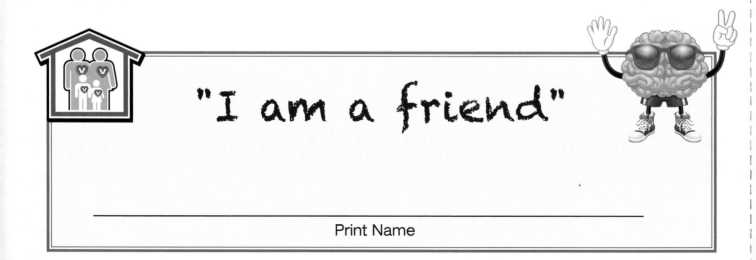

"I am a friend"

_____
Print Name

Use what you know about complimentary angles to determine the measure of angles **a, b, and c** in the figure below.

< a = _____

< b = _____

< c = _____

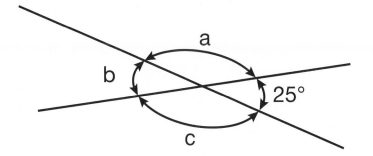

Boston Massacre

The colonies were having differences of opinion with the motherland. England kept taxing the colonists to pay for various wars which they said the colonists benefited from. The colonists felt they were being overtaxed, without benefit of representation to the people making the laws. England tried several different taxes, and the colonists rebelled at each one of them. In 1767 England tried to tax glass, lead, paper and tea. Many people refused to pay the taxes, so England sent soldiers to enforce the laws. This infuriated the people.

In the winter of 1770 some colonists were taunting a group of British soldiers. They threw rocks and snowballs at the soldiers. To stop the harassment, and get some vengeance, the British soldiers fired into the crowd. Four people were killed in what later came to be called the Boston Massacre. Newspapers spread the story throughout the colonies, most with a colonial perspective. The colonists were outraged at the incident, and Britain had to repeal most of the taxes they had set. However, they wanted to send the message that they were still in charge, so they left in place a tax on tea. This led to the Boston Tea Party, in which a group of colonists called the Sons of Liberty, dumped tea from one of the British ships into the harbor.

1. What were 3 of the things the British tried to tax? _____

_____

_____

2. What did the British do to stop the colonists from throwing things at them?

_____

_____

Aerobic

Go to www.summerfitlearning.com for more Activities!

DAILY EXERCISE
Jogging for Fitness 15
"Stretch Before You Play!"

Instruction
Jog 15 minutes in
place or outside

Be Healthy!
Eat more
whole grains
like pasta,
bread and rice.

DAY 1

Apostrophe Use

There are five simple rules for using an apostrophe correctly.

1. Use an apostrophe + s ('s) to show that one person/thing owns or is a member of something.
2. Use an apostrophe after the "s" at the end of a plural noun to show possession.
3. If a plural noun doesn't end in "s," add an "'s" to create the possessive form.
4. When you combine two words to make a contraction, you will always take out some letters. In their place, use an apostrophe.
5. For names ending in s, add apostrophe s ('s).

Use these rules to make the correct choice in each sentence. (Some may not need an apostrophe – be careful.)

1. The (children's , childrens') rooms are usually a bit messy.

2. Did you get to observe (Chantelle's , Chantelles') ballet class?

3. The boys (havent' , haven't) had much practice bowling.

4. The (parent's , parents') classes were held in the evening.

5. Many of the (girl's , girls') dresses were similar in color and style.

6. The children and their (parents', parents) enjoyed the program immensely.

7. Samson collected the other (boys', boys) books for them.

8. Cassie held onto the little (boys', boy's) hand.

9. I will return the (students , students') tests after lunch.

10. Will you please return (Charles' , Charles's) book to him.

Mean, median, and mode are three kinds of averages. The mean is the average where you add up all the numbers and then divide by the number of numbers. The median is the middle value in the list of numbers. To find the median, your numbers have to be listed in numerical order, so you may have to rewrite your list first. If there is no exact middle, take the middle two numbers and find the middle of them (if the middle two numbers are 15 and 18, the middle would be 16.5) The mode is the value that occurs most often. If no number is repeated, then there is no mode for the list. The range is just the difference between the largest and smallest values.

Find the Mean, Median, Mode and Range for the following list of numbers:

13, 18, 13, 14, 13, 16, 14, 21, 13

Mean = _____   Median = _____   Mode = _____   Range = _____

DAY 2

Boiling and Melting Points

Matter can exist in different states. Water can be solid ice, liquid, or gas vapor, but it is still H2O – water. The temperature at which a solid turns into a liquid is called its melting point. The melting point for water is 0 degrees C (32 degrees F). When the opposite happens and a liquid turns into a solid, it is called freezing. For water, the freezing point is also 0 degrees C (32 degrees F).

When a liquid becomes a gas it is called boiling or vaporization. The boiling point for water is 100 degrees C (212 degrees F). When the opposite occurs and a gas becomes a liquid, it is called condensation. Evaporation is liquid becoming a gas; that happens only on the surface of a liquid. Evaporation doesn't always need a high temperature to occur.

Use this chart of the boiling points of some liquids to answer the questions.

Fluid	Boiling point Celsius	Boiling point Fahrenheit
Methyl Alcohol	64.7	151
Ammonia	-35.5	-28.1
Jet fuel	163	325
Olive oil	300	570
Water	100	212

1. Which fluid has the highest boiling point in both scales? _____

2. Which fluid has the lowest boiling point in both scales? _____

3. What is the difference in boiling points between water and olive oil using the
    Fahrenheit scale? _____

4. What is the difference of the same fluids using the Celsius scale? _____

5. What fuel did you think would have the highest boiling point and why? _____

WEEK 10

Strength

DAILY EXERCISE
Planks
"Stretch Before You Play!"

Instruction
Go as long as you can.
Try for 3-4 minutes

Be Healthy!
Learn a new joke today and tell it at dinner.

Vocabulary

DAY 2

WEEK 10

Choose the word or group of words that means the same, or nearly the same, as the underlined word.

1. ___ An overwhelming impulse :
   A. anger   B. urge   C. understanding   D. worry

2. ___ A pleasant reverie:
   A. picture   B. daydream   C. occurrence   D. surprise

3. ___ A tedious assignment:
   A. difficult   B. boring   C. silly   D. daily

4. ___ Deep meditation:
   A. hunger   B. joy   C. reflection   D. sorrow

5. ___ A pile of kindling:
   A. leaves   B. old metal   C. dry wood   D. dirty clothes

6. ___ A blunt response:
   A. abrupt   B. sorrowful   C. comical   D. hurried

7. ___ Inadequate work:
   A. elaborate   B. insufficient   C. excellent   D. simple

8. ___ A sturdy barricade:
   A. bridge   B. gateway   C. garage   D. barrier

9. ___ To improvise:
   A. to decrease   B. to laugh   C. to invent   D. to despair

10. ___ Perpetual:
    A. short term   B. continual   C. broken   D. complete

11. ___ Diminish:
    A. to make greater   B. to deny   C. to lessen   D. to build

12. ___ Perilous journey:
    A. dangerous   B. joyous   C. confusing   D. lengthy

13. ___ Conspiracy:
    A. disagreement   B. battle   C. secret plan   D. party

14. ___ Commence:
    A. enjoy   B. end   C. continue   D. begin

In the real world events cannot be predicted with absolute certainty. Instead, we try to decide how likely they are to happen, using the idea of probability. If a coin is tossed in the air, there are two possibilities as to how it will land – heads or tails. We express this as a one in two chance, or the probability is ½. Try to figure out the following probabilities.

1. Harry's school is having a raffle. First prize is a basket of goodies. There are 200 tickets sold. Harry buys 4 tickets. What is the probability of him winning the first prize?

2. What is the probability of choosing a green marble from a jar containing 5 red, 6 green and 4 blue marbles?

3. What is the probability of choosing a jack or a queen from a standard deck of 52 playing cards?

Lexington and Concord

In the poem *The Midnight Ride of Paul Revere*, Henry Wadsworth Longfellow recounts events leading to the Lexington and Concord conflict.

American colonists had been stockpiling weapons in the city of Concord, Massachusetts. The British troops who were stationed in Boston marched on Concord to seize the weapons. Revere and two other men, William Dawes and Dr. Samuel Prescott, rode to warn the patriots that the British were headed their way. Though Revere is honored in Longfellow's poem, only Prescott actually made it to warn the colonists. Revere and Dawes were both stopped by British patrols. On the way to Concord, the British went through Lexington. No one is certain who fired the first shot, but it has been called "The Shot Heard Round the World". This is because the British Empire had colonies all around the world and this shot affected all of the British Empire. At any rate, both sides opened fire, and the Americans were forced to withdraw. However, they had slowed the British on their march to Concord. By the time the British got to Concord the Americans were waiting. The Americans forced the British back and saved the weapons depot. The Revolutionary War had begun.

True of False

1. _____ Paul Revere was able to warn the colonists at Lexington.

2. _____ William Dawes and Dr. Samuel Prescott rode to warn the colonists, too.

3. _____ The British were victorious in both battles.

4. _____ The battles of Lexington and Concord marked the end of the

    Revolutionary War.

5. _____ The British marched on Concord because the colonists had been stock-

    piling weapons there.

DAY
3

WEEK 10

Aerobic Go to www.summerfitlearning.com for more Activities!

DAILY EXERCISE
Tree Sprints
"Stretch Before You Play!"

Instruction
Perform 3-5 sprints

Cause and Effect

Simply stated the cause is the reason why something occurs, the effect is what occurs.
In each sentence, underline the cause and circle the effect.

1. When Stacey brought in the hot dogs, everyone cheered.

2. Joanne was not hired because she was late for her job interview.

3. We couldn't find the funding, so the band trip was canceled.

4. The picnic was canceled due to the rainstorm that developed.

5. Since Curtis was late, Elizabeth had to go to the play alone.

6. It was snowing outside, so school was canceled.

7. Teddy noticed that if he was around dogs, he sneezed a lot.

8. Because they had extra money, the children bought a treat.

9. There was ice on the step and Samantha slipped.

10. Due to the rain, the children were forced to play inside.

11. There had been little rain; consequently, the flowers were drooping.

12. You spilled the milk; therefore you clean it up.

13. Cookies and candy are high in sugar, so they are not healthy snacks.

14. He raised enough money that he was able to buy a new bike.

15. In order to join the choir, I will need to free up my Thursday afternoons.

16. He stayed up late last night, so Frankie is having trouble staying awake today.

17. The television was too loud, so Mother went to read in the kitchen.

18. After the party, the whole house needed cleaning.

19. Patricia was learning the guitar, so she decided to enter the talent show.

20. Since the last sentence is finished, you may now rest.

Earlier in this book we looked at the area of a cube, which would be how much material you would need to cover the cube. Now we will look at the volume of a cube – how much you can fill it with. Use the formula V cube = a3 where a is the measure of a side. Be sure to label your answer as cu. cm.

1. If a =3, V = _____

2. If a =7, V = _____

3. If a =6, V = _____

4. If a = 2.5, V = _____

5. If a = 4.6, V = _____

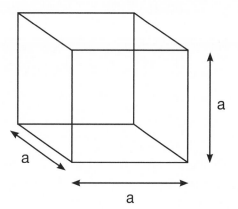

Formation of precipitate

A precipitate forms from a chemical reaction because the substances are insoluble. Since they are insoluble, they form a solid, which is the precipitate. Rock Candy is a great example.

Water (a solvent) dissolves sugar (a solute) to create what chemists call a solution. Under normal conditions, a fixed amount of water can only dissolve a certain amount of sugar before it becomes saturated. When you make rock candy, you boil a sugar-water solution over high heat. The heat increases the amount of sugar that the water can dissolve to create a super-saturated solution. Super-saturated solutions are unstable, so when you stir rock candy, sugar crystals will come out of the solution and attach to the string or stick in the jar. This process is called precipitation. The sugar crystals are called precipitates.

Dissolve 3 cups of sugar in 2 cups of boiling water on the stove top. Keep the water boiling while you stir with a wooden spoon to make sure all of the sugar is dissolved.

Allow the liquid to cool, then pour the sugar water into a jar or other heat-proof receptacle.

Drop a wooden or bamboo skewer into the jar. Trim the skewer if it protrudes from the lid of the jar. Cover the jar with a paper towel and secure it with a rubber band. This keeps dust and bugs out. Place the jar in the sunlight.

Wait two weeks for crystals to form on the bamboo stick.

DAY 4

WEEK 10

DAILY EXERCISE
Chin-ups
"Stretch Before You Play!"

Instruction
Repeat 2 times

Be Healthy!
Smoking is one of the worst things you can do to your body.

DAY
4

WEEK 10

Suffixes

Using what you know about suffix meanings, match each word to its correct meaning.

1. ___ joyous	A. study of life
2. ___ leaden	B. full of joy
3. ___ aviator	C. one who instructs
4. ___ biology	D. made of lead
5. ___ teacher	E. not able to believe
6. ___ unbelievable	F. one who flies
7. ___ appendectomy	G. in a gentle manner
8. __ gently	H. cutting out of an appendix
9. ___ fearless	I. study of the heart
10. ___ government	J. not frightened
11. ___ terrorist	K. afraid of night
12. ___ cardiology	L. state of governing
13. ___ spheroid	M. one who frightens others
14. ___ geology	N. study of the earth
15. ___ noctiphobia	O. shape of a circle

More homophones and other common errors

In English, many words sound the same but are spelled differently and have different meanings. These are called homophones. You can use the context of a sentence to decide which word is appropriate to use.

There are also words that people commonly misuse, such as then and than.
Circle the correct words in each sentence.

1. You begin the name of a (capital , capitol) city with a (capital , capitol) letter.
2. He was sadder (than , then) could be, and (than , then) he got his present.
3. Connor had felt very (week , weak) this past (week , weak).
4. "We have gone (farther , further) than we needed to," Ruby complained (farther , further).
5. "Your victory is in the (passed , past)," crowed Nate as he (passed , past) Emilio.
6. His speech made an (allusion , illusion) to the magician's (allusion , illusion).
7. As the couple stood at the (alter , altar) they were glad they did not (altar, alter) their plans.
8. He was very (horse , hoarse) from yelling to his (horse , hoarse).
9. Tony was (quiet , quite) certain the children were being (quiet , quite).
10. Are you sure (you're , your) doing (you're , your) math correctly?

FRIENDSHIP - J. R. R. Tolkien and C. S. Lewis

J. R. R. Tolkien was born in South Africa, but his family returned to their native England after his father died. He showed an early interest in languages and studied at Oxford. He later became a professor there. He wrote many books, poems, and other works, but his most famous are *The Hobbit* (which began as a story for his children) and the *Lord of the Rings Trilogy*.

C. S. Lewis is known for the *Narnia Chronicles*, though he wrote many other books as well. He was born in Northern Ireland, but when he was 10, he was sent to school in England. He also studied at Oxford and later became a professor there.

Tolkien and Lewis met each other at a faculty meeting when they both taught at Oxford University in England. They both loved mythology, and believed that myths and legends were a way to communicate deeper truths and values. As many friends do, they frequently disagreed – about philosophies, methods of writing, and the messages their writings gave to readers. But also, as friends do, they agreed to disagree, they embraced each other's differences, and enjoyed the time they were able to be together.

1. What does this story teach you about friends having different opinions? _____

_____

_____

2. What books did Lewis write? _____

_____

3. What books did Tolkien write? _____

_____

_____

_____

4. What things did Tolkien and Lewis both enjoy or believe? _____

_____

_____

_____

Color a star for each time you show Friendship through your own actions this week.

 Write a 50-75 word essay describing one of your Friendship actions this week.

Friendship – Memorize Your Value

"Wherever we are, it is our friends that make our world."

– Henry Drummond

Core Value Booklist
Read More About Friendship

Charlotte's Web
By E.B. White

The Hundred Dresses
By Eleanor Estes-Louis Slobodkin

Because of Winn Dixie
By Kate DiCamillo

········**TECH TIME!**··········

It can be fun to figure out what a person is expressing by listening to sounds or music that he or she has put together. You can do this with provided sounds and music from various online tools. Make a creation that musically represents friendship. Make sure your friends get to hear it.

www.SummerFitLearning.com

Bill Gates
Tech Guru and
Philanthropist
gatesfoundation.org

Play Time!
Choose a Game or Activity to Play for 60 minutes today!

YOU CHOOSE

_____
Write down which game or activity you played today!

Be Healthy!
You may have a favorite food, but it's best to eat a variety.

WEEK 10

DAY 5

1 2 3

EXTRAS
**Fitness Index
Family Health and Wellness Tips
Summer Journal • Book Report
Answer Key • Certificate of Completion**

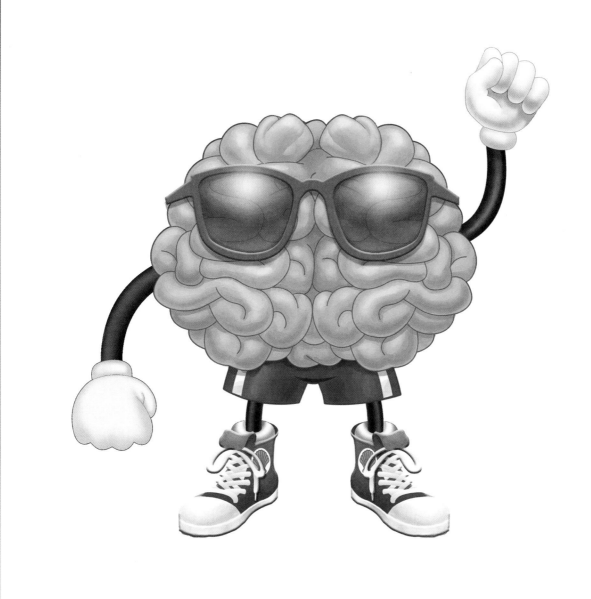

FITNESS INDEX

A healthy life is an active life. Kids need to be physically active for 60 minutes a day. Use the daily fitness activity to get moving. After 10 weeks of physical activity you have created a new and healthy lifestyle!

AEROBIC   STRENGTH   SPORTS

Aerobic Exercise = Oxygen

The word "Aerobic" means "needing or giving oxygen." These *Summer Fit* exercises get the heart pumping and oxygen moving to help burn off sugars and calories!

Strength Exercise = Muscle

Strength exercises help make muscles stronger. These *Summer Fit* exercises help build strong muscles to support doing fun activities around the house, school and outdoors!

Play Exercise = Sport Activity

Playing a different sport each week is an opportunity to use the *Summer Fit* oxygen and fitness exercises in a variety of ways. There are a lot of sports to choose from and remember that the most important thing about being *Summer Fit* is to have fun and play!

Warm Up Before Exercising

1 **Inchworm** – Put your hand on the ground in front of your feet. Walked out on the hands and then walk up on the feet. Do this 5 times.

2 **Knee Hug** – While you are slowly walking, pull your knee to your chest and hug. Do this 5 times on each leg.

3 **Toe Grab** – Toe Touch. Grab the toe behind your leg then touch the opposite toe with your opposite hand. Stand up and switch. Repeat 5 tines on each leg.

Warning:

Before starting any new exercise program you should consult your family physician. Even children can have medical conditions and at risk conditions that could limit the amount of physical activity they can do. So check with your doctor and then

Get Fit!

Aerobic Exercise = Oxygen

Aerobic exercises get you moving. When you move your heart pumps faster and more oxygen gets to your lungs. Movement helps burn off sugars and calories and gets you fit!

◆ **Jump the Line:** Use tape on a floor or chalk on cement to create a line. Jump front to back or side-to-side keeping feet together. **Goal = Jump 10 - 15 times back and forth**

◆ **Crooked Bunny:** Use 5 or more sticks, poles, or markers. Line them up leaving 2-3 feet space between each of them. Jump over each line traveling sideways over and back (right to left). **Goal = 3 - 5 times**

◆ **Burpies:** This is full body exercise is performed in four steps. Begin in a standing position. Drop into a squat position with your hands on the ground. Extend your feet back in one quick motion to assume so your body is straight. Return to the squat position in one quick motion. Return to standing position. **Goal = 5 - 7 times**

◆ **Side Shuffles:** Start with feet apart (parallel with one another). Jump up as high as you can and click together mid- air, landing apart in almost a partial squat, and continuing moving sideways in motion left and then right. **Goal = 10 shuffles to the right and 10 shuffles to the left**

◆ **Single Leg Pop-Hops:** Jump forward using only one leg in a continuous hopping motion and attempting to keep balance at the same time, jump back. **Goal = Jump on each leg 10 - 15 times**

◆ **Ladders:** Create 3 to 5 points of reference using different objects as markers to run and touch before returning back to starting position each time. Create different distances by moving your markers or reference points. **Goal = Run your course 3 times**

◆ **Let's Roll:** Put your lungs to work on your bike, skates or scooter. Don't forget to wear helmets and pads!

◆ **Speed:** Rest in between each block. See how fast you and your friends can run for one block. Time yourself and see if you can beat your original time. **Goal = Run 3 blocks**

◆ **Pass and Go:** This activity requires a second person. Ask a friend or someone from your family to play with you. The object of this activity is to pass the ball/bean bag back and forth counting by 2's get to a 100 as fast as you can. Have a stopwatch handy. Set a time you want to beat and go! Increase your goal by setting a lower time. **Goal = Beat your best time!**

◆ **Capture the Flag/ Get Your Family and Friends to Play:** Use scarves or old T-shirts for flags. Use a different color one for each team. Use chalk, cones, tape, or landmarks such as trees or sidewalks to divide your playing area into equal-sized territories for each team. Place one flag into each territory. It must be visible and once it is placed it cannot be moved. When the game begins, players cross into opposing teams' territories to grab their flags. When a player is in an opposing team's territory he/she can be captured by that team's players. If they tag him/her, he/she must run to the sideline and perform an exercise—for example, five jumping jacks or three push-ups. After they perform their exercise the player can go back to his/her own team's territory and resume play. The game ends when one team successfully captures the flag(s) from the other team or teams and returns to their own territory with the opposing team's flag.

◆ **Mountain Climbers:** Start in a pushup position on your hands and toes. Bring your right knee in towards your chest, resting the foot on the floor. Jump up and switch feet in the air, bringing your left foot in and your right foot back. You can also run the knees in and out rather than touching the toes to the floor. Continue alternating your feet as fast as you safely can for 30-60 seconds. **Goal = 3 times for 60 seconds each**

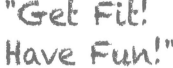

"Get Fit! Have Fun!"

- **Moguls:** Start in an extended plank/pushup position, jump so that your hands stay in place and your feet remain close together, but are moving as far to each side as they can. Jump left to right. **Goal = 3x's for 30 seconds**

- **Racing Leap-Frog:** In leapfrog there are two positions: the squatter and the leaper. Each player rotates these positions throughout the game. The squatter bends his knees and puts his hands firmly on the ground in front of him. His arms are placed between his knees and his head is tucked into his chest, mimicking a frog-like position. The leaper jumps over the squatter by placing her hands on his shoulders and pushing off the ground with her legs to leap over the squatter. Except for having her hands on the squatter's shoulders, the leaper should not touch the squatter while leaping over him. When playing leapfrog with two people, each person immediately rotates between being the leaper and squatter. Move in a forward motion placing hands either behind your head or out in front (to aid in creating distance) 10-15 total leaps could easily be used as a racing method.

- **Bear Crawl:** Find a large open space or a clear path. Start on your hands and feet and move forward just like a bear. Your knees should be slightly bent in order to keep your butt low and even with or slightly higher than your head. Your back should be relatively flat. Brace your abs and keep your head up or slightly neutral to see where you are going!
  Goal = Crawl for 2 - 3 minutes

- **Towel Slide/Plate Push:** Use this exercise for intervals using an object that can slide across the ground or floor. The exercise is simply to keep a firm grip on object and run it down to the other end of the room and back as quickly as possible…this can be done in many places including your backyard on the grass, in your driveway and a gymnasium. **Goal = Complete 5 times**

- **Jump Rope:** is the primary tool used in the game of skipping where you jump over a rope swung so that it passes under your feet and over your head. Here are some different jumps that you can do: **Goal = 3 - 5 minutes without stopping**
  Basic jump or easy jump: This is where both feet are slightly apart and jump at the same time over the rope. Beginners should master this technique first before moving onto more advanced techniques.
  Alternate foot jump (speed step): This style consists of using alternate feet to jump off the ground. This technique can be used to effectively double the number of skips per minute as compared to the above technique. This step is used for speed events.
  Criss-Cross: This method is similar to the basic jump with the only difference being that while jumping, the left hand goes to the right part of the body and vice versa for the right hand, with arms crossing in front of the body.
  Side Swing: This is a basic technique where the rope passes the side of the skipper's body, without jumping it. Usually the skipper performs a basic jump after a side swing, or a criss-cross.

- **Happy Feet:** Use your feet every chance you get today. Walk to a friend's house, to the store, around the park or wherever it's safe to walk. **Goal = Get your parents to walk with you after dinner**

- **Foot bag (need a hackey-sack)/ Play with friends!:** Gather players in a circle about 4-5 feet across. "Serve" the foot-bag to any player by tossing it gently in their direction waist high. Keep the foot bag in the air using any part of your body except your arms and hands. Pass the foot-bag back and forth around the circle for as many times as you can.

- **Tree Sprints/ Perform 3-5 sprints:** Find two trees that are 15-20 feet apart. Start with your left or right leg touching the base of the tree. On "go" sprint as fast as you can to the opposite tree, touch the tree trunk and sprint back to your start position. Continue sprints until you complete your goal or get tired.

- **Gassers:** Using a space about the width of a football or soccer field run/jog 1/4 of the distance lean down to touch the line or marker used then back to the start line. Immediately run/jog to the half-way point, touch the ground, and back to the start, run/jog 3/4 of the way and back then run/jog all the way and back. Goal = Start with one the first time you do this exercise and then work your way up to see how many you can do.

Summer Fit Tip

The more you workout and play with a partner the more they are likely to stick with it. Find a friend or someone in your family to exercise with everyday.

Marci and Courtney Crozier
Former Contestants of NBC's
The Biggest Loser

Strength Exercise = Muscle

Strength exercises make muscles stronger. When you build strong muscles you are able to lift more, run faster, and do fun activities around your house, school, and outdoors!

◆ **Inchworm:** This is a great way to develop strength, coordination, and flexibility. Kneel on the grass or other soft floor surface and stretch forward as far as you can while balancing yourself with your hands, palms down. Your hands and feet should be shoulder width apart. Raise your butt high and bend your head downward so you can see the heels of your feet. Slowly walk your hands until they are touching your feet. **Goal = 10 - 15 times**

◆ **Chair/bench Squats:** Try to keep your back up straight without leaning over too much, squat down and touch the chair with your butt (don't sit) and immediately come back up. **Goal = 5 to 10 times**

◆ **Ninja Crawl/ Crawl for 5 minutes:** Try to maintain a mostly flat back without straining. Keep your weight balanced equally on all four of your limbs. Don't sit too far back on your feet, and don't lean too far forward on your hands. Find a comfortable position that you can hold for a long time. Try to crawl with very little effort. Focus on your exhale, breath calm and slow. Try to crawl softly, quietly – move like a ninja. Try crawling on grass and sand– on flat and hilly surfaces. Crawl sideways, but keeping hands and feel on ground the entire time…aim for distance, longevity, and constant motion heading both right and left directions.

◆ **Dead Bug:** Sit upright and balance on your duff! All your limbs in the air (legs and arms) and balance as long as you can! **Goal = Hold for 2 minutes!**

◆ **One-legged Stand Ups:** Sit in the chair and come up on one leg 10 times (don't use the other leg!), then switch! **Goal = 10 times each leg**

◆ **Grasshopper Crunch:** Start by lying flat on your back, extend one leg and the opposite arm simultaneously, and crunch so that they come as close together as possible in meeting in the middle, then extend back out and return to starting position. **Goal = Complete 7 - 10 for each side**

◆ **Leg Lifts/ Repeat 5 times:** Start by laying flat on your back. Put your hands under your butt, right below your waist, palms down. This will keep your tailbone just off of ground. Raise your legs until they are just off of the ground. During the exercise, your feet must never touch the ground. Your goal is to you're your stomach tight and your legs as straight as you can during the exercise. Raise your legs as high as you can while keeping your knees straight. Lower your legs to their starting position. **Goal = 5 to 7 times**

◆ **Knee lifts:** Stand with your feet flat on the floor. Start by lifting your right knee up 5 times, always bring both feet together between each interval then change legs. When you feel more confident, bounce while you bring your knee up and alternate between legs. **Goal = 5 times each leg**

◆ **Chin-ups:** These are difficult because they use weaker arm and back muscles. From a hanging position, pull yourself up with your torso straight. Use your arms, without twisting your back. Try to raise yourself until your chest is at or near the bar. Hold for one or two seconds then lower yourself down slowly. **Goal = 3 to 5 times**

◆ **Heel Raises:** Heel raises strengthen the calf muscles. Stand with your feet a few inches apart, with your hands lightly resting on a counter or chair in front of you. Slowly raise your heels off the floor while keeping your knees straight. Hold for 5 seconds and then slowly lower your heels to the floor. Repeat. **Goal = Repeat 7 to 10 times**

- **Squats:** Start by placing your hands on your hips and stand with feet about shoulder width apart. Slowly move downward by bending your knees and keeping body straight by sticking out your butt. Squat as far down as you comfortably can, then slowly rise back up until you are standing straight. **Goal = 7 to 10 times**

- **Lunges:** Start by standing with your two feet shoulder length apart with your back straight and your arms by your sides. Simply lunge forward on one knee, count to two and then step back to your original position. After two counts lunge forward on your alternate foot. Always make sure that your front knee never goes beyond your toes. Make sure you keep your balance so you do not fall forward or to the side!
Goal = 5 times each leg

- **Push-ups (traditional or modified):** Practice getting your body into a straight position required for a pushup, by stiffening your body like a flat board. Get on the floor and rest on both forearms and toes, with your body stiff and straight off the floor. Keep your butt down without letting it droop towards the floor so it is straight with the rest of your body. When you are ready to start, take your forearms off the floor and place your hands where they were. Lower your body straight down until your chest almost touches the floor, and then push back up into your straight position. Keep your head up and look straight ahead. **Goal = 7 to 10 times**

  To do a modified push up, get in your straight position and then rest on your knees. When you are ready to start, lower your body straight down while rocking forward on your knees to help take away some of your body weight. Push back up so you are in your original position. This is a great way to start learning push-ups and building your strength.

- **Crunches:** Start by sitting down on the floor, then bend your knees while moving your feet toward your butt. Keep your back and feet flat on the floor. Put your hands behind your head, or arms together in front of your body with your hands tucked under your chin. With your shoulders off the ground as the starting position, raise your head to your knees, using only core muscles. Then lower your body, keeping your shoulders slightly off the ground in the starting position. Try to keep your lower back on the floor and do not use your arms to pull yourself up. **Goal = 5 to 10 times**

- **Chop n Squat:** Start with legs wide, bring your feet together, then out wide again, reach down and touch the ground, and pop up. **Goal = 10 to 12 times**

- **Side Step:** Lung out to your right. Back leg straight, bend the right knee. Slid back and bend the left knee and straighten the right leg. Turn and face the opposite direction and repeat. **Goal = 5 times in each direction**

- **Balance:** Balance on one foot. Foot extended low in front of you. Foot extended low in back of you. Foot extended low to the side. **Goal = Hold for 15 seconds each leg, then switch and repeat 5 - 7 times**

- **Toe Taps:** Start by standing with your two feet shoulder length apart with your back straight and your arms by your sides. While jumping straight up, bring one toe forward to the front and tap while alternating to the opposite foot. Go back and forth between your left and right foot. Find a rhythm and be careful not to lose your balance! **Goal = Repeat 10 times with each foot**

- **Plank:** On the floor get on your stomach, get up on your elbows and have the elbows line up under you shoulders. Lift your body and legs off the floor and you are up on your toes. Hold this for 30 seconds to a minute. **Goal = increase each week with the goal of 2 to 4 minutes at the end**

Exercise Activities for Kids

Find What You Like

Everybody has different abilities and interests, so take the time to figure out what activities and exercises you like. Try them all: soccer, dance, karate, basketball, and skating are only a few. After you have played a lot of different ones, go back and focus on the ones you like! Create your own ways to be active and combine different activities and sports to put your own twist on things. Talk with your parents or caregiver for ideas and have them help you find and do the activities that you like to do. Playing and exercising is a great way to help you become fit, but remember that the most important thing about playing is that you are having fun!

List of Exercise Activities

Home–Outdoor:

Walking
Ride Bicycle
Swimming
Walk Dog
Golf with whiffle balls outside
Neighborhood walks/Exploring (in a safe area)
Hula Hooping
Rollerskating/Rollerblading
Skateboarding
Jump rope
Climbing trees
Play in the back yard
Hopscotch
Stretching
Basketball
Yard work
Housecleaning

Home – Indoor:

Dancing
Exercise DVD
Yoga DVD
Home gym equipment
Stretch bands
Free weights
Stretching

With friends or family:

Red Rover
Chinese jump rope
Regular jump rope
Ring around the rosie
Tag/Freeze
Four score
Capture the flag
Dodgeball
Slip n Slide
Wallball
Tug of War
Stretching
Run through a sprinkler
Skipping
Family swim time
Bowling
Basketball
Hiking
Red light, Green light
Kick ball
Four Square
Tennis
Frisbee
Soccer
Jump Rope
Baseball

Turn off TV Go Outside - PLAY!
Public Service Announcement
Brought to you by Summer Fit

Chill out on Screen Time

Screen time is the amount of time spent watching TV, DVDs or going to the movies, playing video games, texting on the phone and using the computer. The more time you spend looking at a screen the less time you are outside riding your bike, walking, swimming or playing soccer with your friends. Try to spend no more than a couple hours a day in front of a screen for activities other than homework and get outside and play!

Health and Wellness Index
Healthy Family Recipes and Snacks

YOGURT PARFAITS: 01

Prep time: 15 minutes
Cook time: 0
Yield: 4 servings
Good for: all ages, limited kitchen, cooking with kids

Ingredients:
2 cups fresh fruit, at least 2 different kinds (can also be thawed fresh fruit)
1 cup low-fat plain or soy yogurt
4 TBSP 100% fruit spread
1 cup granola or dry cereal

YOGURT PARFAITS: 02

Directions:
Wash and cut fruit into small pieces
In a bowl, mix the yogurt and fruit spread together
Layer each of the four parfaits as follows:
Fruit
Yogurt
Granola (repeat)
Enjoy!
Kids can use a plastic knife to cut soft fruit
Kids can combine and layer ingredients

Tips:
A healthier dessert than ice cream
A healthy part of a quick breakfast

Jen Jacobs
Former Contestant
of NBC's
The Biggest Loser

It is important to teach children at a young age about the difference between a snack that is good for you versus a snack that is bad for you. It is equally important to teach your kids about moderation and how to eat until they are full, but not to overeat!

SMOOTHIES: 01

Prep time: 5 minutes
Cook time: 0
Yield: 2 servings
Good for: all ages,
limited kitchen, cooking with kids

Ingredients:
1 cup berries, fresh or frozen
4 ounces vanilla low fat yogurt
½ cup 100% apple juice
1 banana, cut into chunks
4 ice cubes

SMOOTHIES: 02

Directions:
Place apple juice, yogurt, berries, and banana in a blender. Cover and process until smooth

While the blender is running, drop ice cubes into the blender one at a time. Process until smooth

Variation:
Add ½ cup of silken tofu or ½ cup of peanut butter for extra protein.

Crunchy, Fruity Cobbler: 01

Prep time: 5 minutes
Cook time: 5 minutes
Yield: 4 servings (1 cup=1 serving)
Good for: all ages of children

Ingredients:
1 (15 ounce) can of sliced peaches, drained*
1 (15 ounce) can of pear halves, drained*
1/4 tsp. of almond or vanilla extract
1/4 tsp. of ground cinnamon
3/4 cup of low-fat granola with rai
*Canned fruit should be packed in

Crunchy, Fruity Cobbler: 02

Directions:
Combine the peaches, pears, extract and cinnamon in a microwave safe bowl. Stir well.
Sprinkle granola over the top.
Cover the bowl with a lid or plastic wrap, leaving a little opening for the steam to escape.
Microwave on high for 5 minutes.
Use potholders to remove the bowl from the microwave.
Let it cool a little, and then eat.

Health and Wellness Vocabulary

In order to teach your children the difference between healthy habits and unhealthy habits it is important to know and understand some of the basic terminology that you may hear in the media and from health experts.

Courtney Crozier
Former Contestant of NBC's *The Biggest Loser*

VOCABULARY

Calorie: A unit of measure of the amount of energy supplied by food.

Fat: It is one of the 3 nutrients (protein and carbohydrates are the other 2) that supplies calories to the body.

Protein: Is one of the building blocks of life. The body needs protein to repair and maintain itself. Every cell in the human body contains protein.

Carbohydrates: The main function is to provide energy for the body, especially the brain and nervous system.

Type 1 Diabetes: A disease characterized by high blood glucose (sugar) levels resulting in the destruction of the insulin-producing cells of the pancreas. This type of diabetes was previously called juvenile onset diabetes and insulin-dependent diabetes.

Type 2 Diabetes: A disease characterized by high blood glucose (sugar) levels due to the body's inability to use insulin normally, or to produce insulin. In the past this type of diabetes was called adult-onset diabetes and non-insulin dependent diabetes.

Sedentary lifestyle: A type of lifestyle with no or irregular physical activity. It pertains to a condition of inaction.

BMI: An index that correlates with total body fat content, and is an acceptable measure of body fatness in children and adults. It is calculated by dividing weight in kilograms by the square of height in meters. BMI is one of the leading indicators in determining obesity.

Obesity: Refers to a person's overall body weight and whether it's too high. Overweight is having extra body weight from muscle, bone, fat and/or water. Obesity is having a high amount of extra body fat.

Fiber: This is not an essential nutrient, but it performs several vital functions. A natural laxative, it keeps traffic moving through the intestinal tract and may lower the concentration of cholesterol in the blood.

Nutrient dense foods: Foods that contain relatively high amounts of nutrients compared to their caloric value.

Screen time: The amount of time a person participates in watching or playing something on a screen. The screen could be a television, computer, computer games, and a variety of electronics that interact with people utilizing a screen of various sizes. The American Academy of Pediatrics recommends no screen time before age 2 and no more that 1-2 hours of screen time for children over age 2.

Food label: Information listed inside a square box on prepared food packaging that shows the nutritional value of a product one consumes. It also gives the value shown as a percentage of the daily nutritional values that the Food and Drug Administration (FDA) recommend for a healthy diet.

Serving size: This term is used by the United States Department of Agriculture (USDA) to measure amounts of food. It is a tool for healthy eating.

Fat: is a source of energy. Fats perform many important functions in the body. There are healthy fats and unhealthy fats.

Monounsaturated and polyunsaturated oils: These contain some fatty acids that are HEALTHY. They do not increase the bad cholesterol in the body. Some of the foods in this category include fish, nuts and avocados.

Saturated fat: This "solid" fat increases bad cholesterol which can lead to it building up in the arteries and cause disease, more specifically, heart disease.

Trans fat: This fat is mostly found in processed foods and it contains unhealthy oils (partially hydrogenated). This type of fat has been shown to increase the bad cholesterol in the body and lower the good cholesterol.

Preadolescent: generally is defined as ages 9-11 years of age for girls and 10-12 years for boys.

Middle childhood: generally defines children between the ages of 5 to 10 years of age.

"School age": is another word for middle childhood.

"Tween": a relatively new term for a child between middle childhood and adolescence.

Health and Wellness: Child Nutrition

1. Preadolescent ("tweens") and school age children's growth continues at a steady, slow rate until the growth spurt they will experience in adolescence. Children of this age continue to have growth spurts that usually coincide with increased appetite. Parents should not be overly concerned about the variability and intake of their school-age children.

2. The importance of family mealtimes cannot be stressed enough. There is a positive relationship between families who eat together and the overall quality of a child's diet.

3. Continue to have your child's BMI-for-age percentile monitored to screen for over and underweight.

4. In this age group the choices a child makes about his or her food intake are becoming more and more influenced by their peers, the media, coaches, and teachers. These outside influences steadily increase as a child ages and becomes more independent.

5. School plays a key role in promoting healthy nutrition and physical activity, so try to participate in healthy, school-related activities with your child, such as walk to school days and volunteering in the school's garden club.

6. Limited physical activity, along with sedentary activities are major contributing factors to the sharp increase of childhood obesity.

7. Soft drink or soda consumption, which tends to increase as a child ages, is associated with increased empty caloric intake and an overall poorer diet. These soft drinks also are a major contributor to dental caries. Diet sodas have no nutrient value, though they are not high in calories.

8. Complications from overweight and obesity in childhood and adolescence are steadily rising. This is including type 2 diabetes (usually adult onset diabetes) and high cholesterol levels.

9. Those children in the age ranges of middle childhood and preadolescence are strongly encouraged to eat a VARIETY of foods and increase physical activity to 60 minutes every day. Parents should set a good example by being physically active themselves and joining their children in physical activity.

10. Parents with healthy eating behaviors and are physically active on a regular basis are excellent role models for their children.

Healthy Websites

www.myplate.gov

www.readyseteat.com

www.nourishinteractive.com

www.cdph.ca.gov/programs/wicworks

www.cdc.gov
(food safety practices, childhood diabetes and obesity)

www.who.int

www.championsforchange.net

www.nlm.nih.gov/medlineplus

Healthly Lifestyles Start at Home

Staying active and healthy is important because it will have a positive impact on every aspect of your life.

Jay and Jen Jacobs
Former Contestants of NBC's
The Biggest Loser

1 **Lead by example:** Your children will do what they see you do. Eat your fruits and vegetables, go for walks and read a book instead of watching television. Your child will see and naturally engage in these activities themselves.

2 **Limit Screen Time:** The American Academy of Pediatrics recommends no screen time before age 2 and no more that 1-2 hours of screen time for children over age 2. Instead of limiting screen time for just them, try regulating it as a household. Keep a log of technology time, note "Screen Free Zones" like the bedroom and try shutting off all technology at least 1 day a week.

3 **Talk at the Table:** Sitting down with the family for dinner gives everybody an opportunity to reconnect and share experiences with each other. Limit distractions by not taking phone calls during dinner and turning the television off.

4 **Drink More Water (and milk):** Soda and other packaged drinks are expensive and contain a lot of sugar and calories. Set an example by drinking water throughout the day and encourage your children to drink water or milk when they are thirsty. These are natural thirst quenchers that provide the mineral and nutrients young (and old) bodies really need.

5 **Portion Control:** There is nothing wrong with enjoying food, but try to eat less. Use smaller plates so food is not wasted and teach your children to tell the difference between being satisfied and overeating.

6 **Make Time For Family Play:** Instead of sitting down to watch TV together plan an activity as a family. Go for a walk or bike ride, work on the yard together, visit the neighbor as a family. It's a great way to reduce technology, but more importantly a great opportunity to enjoy time together as a family.

SUMMER JOURNAL

_____

_____

SUMMER JOURNAL

_____

_____

SUMMER JOURNAL

_____

_____

SUMMER JOURNAL

_____

_____

SUMMER JOURNAL

SUMMER JOURNAL

_____

_____

SUMMER JOURNAL

_____

_____

Summer Fit Book Report

Grade 7-8

Title: _____

Author: _____

Main Characters: _____

_____

_____

_____

Most interesting part of the story: _____

_____

_____

_____

_____

Would you recommend this book to another student? Why or why not? _____

_____

_____

Did you like the way the story ended? Why or why not?: _____

_____

_____

Brief Summary: _____

_____

_____

_____

_____

_____

_____

Pretest - Reading
1. c   2. e   3. d   4. b   5. g   6. f   7. a   8. i   9. h
1. c   2. b   3. e   4. a   5. d   6. d   7. a   8. b   9. e   10. c   11. b
12. c   13. a   14. e   15. d   16. c   17. e   18. a   19. b   20. d
1. b   2. space travel or interplanetary shuttle   3. no money to travel
4. tried to get an extra job   5. sell something

Math Pretest Answers
1. 34.45   2. 37.365   3. 799.8   4. 749.54   5. 76.44   6. 82
7. 1.56   8. 88   9. 1 1/3   10. 4/9   11. 16/27   12. 2/3   13. 5 1/2
14. 1 1/6   15. 7 2/9   16. 1 7/13   17. x = 3   18. 37%   19. 9/25
20. 81%   21. n = 5   22. -9   23. -1   24. 5   25. 3   26. -8   27. 2
28. 15   29. -14   30. -48   31. 15   32. -5   33. -7   34. -8
35. 14   36. x > 20   37. x > -2   38. x > 6   39. y < 4   40. 13 = x
41. -14 = x   42. z = 2   43. a = 2   44. t = 8   45. a=6

Exercises
Week 1 Day 1
1. 41 : 36   2. 33 : 15   3. 21 : 15 or 7 : 5   4. 20 : 15 or 4 : 3
5. 21 : 20   Challenge. 20 : 15
Answers will vary. Should indicate that plants in the room with the southern exposure may grow better due to the sunlight.
1. mongoose   2. cobra   3. afraid   4. afraid   5. fight and eat snakes
6. no - "If he had been an old mongoose"   7. Rikki is in conflict with Nag and Nagaina

Week 1 Day 2
1. 3/10   2. 33/50   3. ¼   4. 17/20   5. 12/25   6. 51%   7. 52%
8. 62.5%   9. 70%   10. 100%
1. I   2. D   3. D   4. D   5. I   6. I
1. False   2. True   3. False   4. True   5. True   6. True   7. False   8. True

Week 1 Day 3
1. $29.20   2. $50.16   3. $54.00
Steps 2, 4, 5, 8 should be marked yes; steps 1, 3, 6, 7 should be marked no
1. The Adventures of Tom Sawyer   2. Mark Twain   3. Home, school, church   4. mid 1800s;   Missouri   5. heartache, witnessed a murder

Week 1 Day 4
1) $340   2) $1,172.50   3) $107.78

	Mall	School
Layout	Long hallways	Long hallways
Rooms	Many rooms	Many rooms
What is in rooms	Items for sale	Desks
Purpose of place	Sales	Learning
Who is there	Clerks, shoppers	Teacher, students

Literature   4, 6, 5, 1, 3, 2, 7

Week 1 Day 5
Canesha Blackman   1. Homeless, 5 children, single   2. Answers will vary   3. It would have been tempting to keep the money and use it for her family.   4. Many people have sent money and gifts to her.

Week 2 Day 1
1. 240 inches
1. people, animals, goods, ideas   2. people and animals   3. Ideas
1. depth and breadth   2. I love thee   3. purely, praise

Week 2 Day 2
1. 1/4   2. 38/1000 or 19/500   3. 33/100   4. 4 3/25
5. 2 11/50   6. 4 3/4   7. 1 1/10   8. 2 1/2
1. is a simile.
1. I   2. I   3. Dad said, "Would you please stop annoying your sister?"
4. The football team shouted in unison, "Go, Ramblers!!"   5. Nathan Hale said, "I regret that I have but one life to give for my country."
6. I   7. I
1. C   2. C   3. X   4. X   5. C   6. X   7. C   8. C

Week 2 Day 3
1. 78%   2. 50%   3. 35%   4. 72%   5. 125%   6. 63%
7. 395%   8. 510%
1. use as fertilizer   2. renews forest resources, provides animal habitats, strengthens ozone layer   3. destroys ozone, animal habitats, resources   4. to preserve or save something
1. name or family; change his name   2. The name doesn't affect who you really are   3. a rose   4. Answers will vary

Week 2 Day 4
1. 1 17/100   2. 2 13/20   3. 1 ¾   4. 4 19/20   5. 1 ½   6. 2 8/25
7. 3 16/25   8. 1 9/20
1. mow lawn   2. Wherever people go they leave their mark
3. Answers will vary
1. her heart was hard like a stone   2. her voice was as pleasant as music   3. life has lots of ups, downs, twists, turns like a roller coaster
4. the office kept him locked up inside   5. Selena was very good, like angels   6. the noise the children made was as pleasant as music
7. the business world is complicated and difficult to get through like a jungle   8. the runner was as fast as a gazelle   9. education opens opportunities like a gate opens into a space
1. act of blocking   2. written after   3. informed wrongly   4. thought about before   5. study of life   6. writing about one's own life
7. writing about someone else's life

Week 2 Day 5
Eleanor Roosevelt   1. Any two: the poor, women's rights, children's causes, racial equality, and human rights   2. One sent to represent others at a meeting, convention or gathering 3. Answers will vary

Week 3 Day 1
1. -8   2. 6   3. 6   4. -16   5. 7   6. -3   7. 2   8. -9   9. 11   10. 6
1. whom   2. who   3. who   4. who   5. whom
6. who   7. whom   8. who   9. who   10. whom
1. gold   2. strong workers, keep men warm   3. kingly   4. gambling and losing   5. wife and children   6. sold to the North by Manuel

Week 3 Day 2
1. -4   2. 1   3. 2   4. -13   5. 17   6. 3   7. -18   8. 10   9. 18   10. -10
Answers will vary
1. a   2. b   3. a   4. b   5. b   6. a   7. b   8. b
1. adjective   2. adverb   3. adverb   4. adverb   5. adverb   6. adjective
7. adverb   8. adverb   9 adverb   10. adjective   11. adverb   12. adverb

Week 3 Day 3
1. 30,340   2. -9   3. -350   4. $29
1. depend   2. Variety of plants and animals exist there   3. Answers will vary
1. order   2. keep   3. corrupt   4. moody   5. grotesque   6. enticing
7. critical   8. retire   9. stir   10. compliment   11. farewell   12. gradual
1. stormy   2. whole   3. ridiculous   4. satisfied   5. open   6. wintery
7. keep   8. relax   9. partner   10. calm   11. cowardly   12. strong
13. nimble   14. pessimist

Week 3 Day 4
1. 12   2. -40   3. -35   4. 21   5. 0   6. -16   7. 30   8. -36   9. 28   10. -28
1. Pull   2. Pull   3. Push   4. Push   5. Push   6. Pull
1. tell the truth or lie   2. watch TV or study   3. steal or not   4. which friend to go with   5. go to the party or go home   6. tell on Sean or not

Week 3 Day 5
Dana Reeve   1. Accidental fall while riding a horse   2. Not able to move   3. Help improve the daily lives of people living with paralysis
4. Answers will vary

Week 4 Day 1
Area = 615.44 cm   Circumference = 87.92 cm
2. weather, affect   2. your, weird   3. a lot, their   4. passed, then
5. past, effect   6. whether, a lot   7. its, you're   8. weather, effect
9. than   10. their
1. Answers will vary

Week 4 Day 2
486 cu. cm
abcbdb
1. I   2. D "Anastasia is late for supper again," said Fredrick.
3. I   4. D The boys said, "Suzanne is the best babysitter we've had."
5. D "We can listen to the new CD in the car," said Cheryl.   6. I   7. I
8. I   9. I   10. D Agnes smiled and said, "I know the correct answer.''
1. iron and nickel   2. under the continents   3. the crust

Week 4 Day 3
16.5 cm
1. sitting on the river bank reading   2. the rabbit talked, wore a waistcoat, and had a watch   3. she was curious about the rabbit
1. hydropower   2. Honduras   3. Answers will vary   4. Information about resources is not enough to make accurate inferences about economy

Week 4 Day 4
1. $(8 \times 70) + (8 \times 6) = 608$

2. $\dfrac{14}{21} \times \dfrac{36}{18} = \dfrac{2 \times 7 \times 3 \times 3 \times 2 \times 2}{3 \times 7 \times 2 \times 3 \times 3} = \dfrac{2}{2} \times \dfrac{7}{7} \times \dfrac{3}{3} \times \dfrac{3}{3} \times \dfrac{2}{3} \times \dfrac{2}{3} = \dfrac{4}{3}$

1. clock   2. magazines   3. chair   4. coffee   5. guitar strings
6. food   7. book   8. order   9. windshield   10. flowers
1. patience, patients   2. peeling, peal   3. hanger, hangar
4. least, leased   5. morning, mourning   6. sore, soar
7. bare, bear   8. tacks, tax   9 grayed, grade
10. adds, ads   11. need, knead   12. fare, fair
1. grandmother   2. sister   3. Julio   4. crew   5. me
6. nurses   7. Paula   8. patrons   9. horses   10. Christine

Week 4 Day 5
Kristi Yamaguchi   1. She had to break bad skating habits in order to do better at dancing   2. She worked for long periods of time to improve her skills   3. Children of all abilities can play on the playgrounds together   4. Her older sister skated and it was recommended as physical therapy for her

Week 5 Day 1
1. z = -32   2. a = 8   3. a = 11   4. a = 25
1. C   2. A   3. Answers will vary
1. true   2. false   3. false   4. true   5. false   6. true

Week 5 Day 2
1. yes   2. yes   3. no   4. yes   5. no
1. Euro   2. Russia   3. Greek and Roman civilizations were the beginnings of democracy
1. gloomy   2. dreary, weak, weary   3. rapping and tapping
4. rare and radiant   5. She has died

Week 5 Day 3

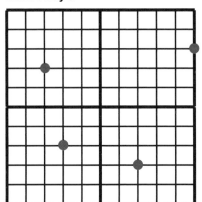

1. centimeters   2. horizontally   3. vertically
4. Pacific   5. earthquakes   6. Volcanoes
Joseph and Helen were going on a picnic. They were happy to be getting away from school and work for awhile. Helen packed a great picnic basket. Joseph had helped her to make several kinds of sandwiches. They had put in some chips, soda, napkins, and paper plates. They even had some fudge for dessert. When they got everything ready, they headed for the door. But to their dismay, the overcast sky began to drip raindrops on everything. At first, Joseph and Helen were disappointed, but then they thought they could still have the picnic – on the living room floor! It was a great picnic!
1. pleassure   2. instaed   3. greif   4. amoung   5. reletive   6. caried
7. apoint   8. soldire   9. diamand   10. advize   11. arguement
12. amusment   13. atorney   14. eleberate

Week 5 Day 4
1) $371.25   2) $4265.40   3) 13%
1. the engine wheezed   2. pizza was arguing   3. flame danced
4. light conquered   5. party died   6. winter had a grip   7. city sleeps
8. birds played a game   9. sunlight sneaked   10. wind sang   11. sun was glaring   12. wind had arms   13. door protested   14. flowers bent their heads   15. éclairs called
1. this   2. those   3. those   4. this   5. those   6. these   7. these   8. those   9 that   10. that
1. diverse   2. populous   3. Kilimanjaro   4. Victoria   5. Mediterranean
6. hippopotamus   7. rhinoceros   8. Savannah

Week 5 Day 5
Pele   1. change   2. children   3. orphanage   4. He had a very rough childhood himself

Week 6 Day 1
1. 60%   2. 66%
1. Europe and Africa   2. China   3. So big that many different cultures developed
1 – 8 Answers will vary
9. feet hurt a lot   10. very tired   11. computer is very old   12. Jacqui will be back very soon.

Week 6 Day 2
1. -17; 1/17   2. 32; -1/32   3. -1/4; 4   4. -3/5; 5/3   5. -7/10; 10/7
Answers will vary
1. Began   2. Grown   3. Ride   4. Spoke   5. Find
6. Got   7. Rung   8. Threw   9. Write   10. Forgiven

Week 6 Day 3
1. 117   2. 50   3. 50   4. 23   5. 55   6. 8   7. 47   8. 45   9. 20   10. 90
1. his father was dying   2. cold   3. the beach   4. he was missing two fingers   5. doesn't like the captain   6. says he is an unpleasant guest
1. home to some of the world's most unique animals and plants 2. Inca
Semicolon after these words: 1. outside   2. tomorrow   3. Italy
4. drums   5. evening   6. trip   7. Beatles   8. watercolors   9. again
10. cake

Week 6 Day 4
1. x = 3   2. x = 15   3. x = -11   4. x = 1   5. x = 5
6. x = 2   7. x = 2   8. x = 5   9. x = 3   10. x = 7
1. heat and pressure   2. chemicals
1. Canada, United States and Mexico   2. Spain   3. Spanish
1. successful   2. weather   3. sincerely   4. government
5. environment   6. forty   7. surprised   8. library   9. unforgettable
10. valuable   11. embarrass   12. recognize   13. appearance
14. professor   15. happily

Week 6 Day 5
Teddy Draper Sr.   1. Of the utmost importance   2. You need to send messages without the other side knowing what information you are sending   3. Retrieve   4. Success   5. Answers will vary

Week 7 Day 1
1. 2012   2. January 2010   3. May 2012   4. March 2010
1. water   2. blanket   3. flashlight   4. jacket   5. radio   6. batteries
1. worldly lore   2. puts the llama to work   3. languishing (llanguishing)
4. don't spell your name in a silly way

Week 7 Day 2
1. March 1990   2. April 2000   3. 3.5 inches   4. 2.5 inches
1. desert   2. Australia
Colon after the following words: 1. states   2. dance   3. acceptance
4. rule   5. committee   6. here   7. test   8. person   9. well   10. friends

Week 7 Day 3
1) Answers will vary – should be 2 angles connected by a center ray
Science – no answer needed
Underline the second and third paragraph and sentences one through four in paragraph four

Week 7 Day 4
1) No   2) No   3) Yes   4) No   5) Yes   6) Yes
1. d   2. a   3. e   4. c   5. b
Answers will vary

Week 7 Day 5
Dalai Lama   1. compassion, forgiveness, tolerance, contentment, self-discipline   2. getting along well together   3. The Chinese government has oppressed the Tibetan people   4. Respect one another and recognize the value of each others' traditions

Week 8 Day 1
1. 4   2. 49   3. 36   4. 64   5. 9   6. 81   7. 5   8. 6   9. 9   10. 7
1. Down   2. Hand   3. Square   4. Veins   5. Window   6. Book
7. Poem   8. Fire   9. Write   10. Bookcase   11. Lungs   12. Spider
13. Color   14. Brought   15. Fly
1. first voyage around the world   2. Answers will vary
1. A   2. A   3. A   4. N   5. N   6. A   7. N   8. A   9. A   10. A

Week 8 Day 2
1. Rational   2. Rational   3. Rational   4. Rational   5. Irrational
6. Irrational
1. severe heat waves, hurricanes, lose water, limit electricity, loss of animals   2. reduce waste, conserve water and energy, walk, plant a tree, buy local produce, talk about it
1. First   2. Third   3. First   4. Second   5. First   6. Third
7. Third   8. Second

Week 8 Day 3
1. 3.23 x 10⁶   2. 1 x 10⁹   3. 1.3 x 10⁻⁷   4. 4.5 x 10⁻³   5. 4,560,000
6. 23,000   7. 0.0023   8. 0.0000761
1. needed wood for ships   2. wanted children to be ale to read the Bible
Commas after   1. Kendra, Sandra   2. puppy, cat   3. delicious, nutritious, colorful   4. Indianapolis, Lafayette   5. surprising, unusual, vivid   6. potatoes, onions, carrots   7. wind, dropped   8. skirt, slacks
1. wear warmer clothes, stay indoors   2. body functions slow down, body temperature drops   3. store energy to fuel the body while sleeping

Week 8 Day 4
1. 27   2. 3.375   3. 125   4. 512   5. 32.768   6. 729   7. 3   8. 2
1. 1 from each parent   2. 19   3. brown   4. b and b or blue and blue
1. P   2. A, The grass in the meadow was eaten by the cows.
3. P   4. A, The semi on the freeway was passed by the truck pulling the boat   5. P
1. known   2. frozen   3. began   4. stolen   5. torn   6. knew
7. chosen   8. rang   9. chosen   10. worn

Week 8 Day 5
Rachel Carson   1. Chemicals sprayed on foods to control insects;
they can be harmful to humans as well   2. conservation, agricultural,
resources, responsibility   3. Answers will vary

Week 9 Day 1
1. -8   2. 6   3. -3   4. 10   5. 5   6. 3   7. 3   8. -1   9. 9   10. 3
1. She describes the sun to them in great detail.
2. Sometimes the instructions are on the front and sometimes they are
on the back.
1. injuries   2. leaves   3. rotten   4. change   5. sitting
6. really bad   7. serious   8. said yes

Week 9 Day 2
1. (1,8) (2,10) (3,12)   2. (1,7) (2,9) (3,11)   3. (1,-1) (2,0) (3,1)
1. slave quarters, dairy, laundry, blacksmith shops, barns, smokehouse
2. farm tools, lace, dishes
1. advance or forward   2. down   3. underground   4. truly   5. exact
or same   6. over   7. illustrated   8. foreign   9. harmful   10. possibly
1. d   2. f   3. a   4. e   5. b   6. g   7. c

Week 9 Day 3
Answers will vary. Graph should be a line from bottom left going
through upper right quadrant, passing through points (-2, -1), (0, 3)
and (1, 5)
Use instinct to find their way; go for better climate or for breeding; may
travel in herds, flocks, other groups, or alone; find food along the way,
need particular living conditions
1. Hannah   2. Anna   3. civic   4. solos   5. kayak   6. refer
7. Madam   8. radar   9. repaper   10. sagas   11. yes   12. no
13. yes   14. yes   15. No

Week 9 Day 4
No math answer
Answers will vary
1. yes   2. no   3. yes   4. no   5. no   6. yes   7. yes   8. yes   9. no
10. yes   11. no   12. yes   13. yes   14. yes   15. yes   16. no
17. No   18. Yes

Week 9 Day 5
Sally Ride   1. Go into space   2. Science, math, and technology
3. Coming or happening before   4. Answers will vary. Should discuss
how Ride continued to work for the same goals

Week 10 Day 1
a. 155°   b. 25°   c. 155°
1. Any three: glass, lead, paper, tea   2. fired into the crowd
1. children's   2. Chantelle's   3. haven't   4. parents'   5. girls'
6. parents   7. boys'   8. boy's   9. students'   10. Charles's

Week 10 Day 2
Mean = 15; Median = 14; Mode = 13; Range = 8
1. olive oil   2. ammonia   3. 358°   4. 200°   5. Answers will vary
1. B   2. B   3. B   4. C   5. C   6. A   7. B   8. D   9. C   10. B
11. C   12. A   13. C   14. D

Week 10 Day 3
1. 4/200 or 1/50   2. 6/15 or 2/5   3. 8/52 or 2/13
1. false   2. true   3. false   4. false   5. true
1. Underline "Stacey brought in the hot dogs", circle "everyone
cheered"   2. Underline "she was late for her job interview , circle
"Joanne was not hired"   3. Underline "We couldn't find the funding",
circle "the band trip was canceled"   4. Underline "the rain storm
which developed", circle "the picnic was canceled"   5. Underline
"Curtis was late", circle "Elizabeth had to go to the play alone"   6.
Underline "it was snowing outside", circle "school was canceled"   7.
Underline "if he was around dogs", circle "he sneezed a lot"   8.
Underline "they had extra money", circle "the children bought a treat"
9. Underline "there was ice on the step", circle "Samantha slipped"
10. Underline "rain", circle "the children were forced to play inside"
11. Underline "there had been little rain", circle "the flowers were
drooping"   12. Underline "you spilled the milk", circle "you clean it up"
13. Underline "cookies and candy are high in sugar", circle "they are
not healthy snacks"   14. Underline "he raised enough money", circle
"he was able to buy a new bike"   15. Underline "I will need to free
up my Thursday afternoons", circle "to join the choir"   16. Underline
"he stayed up late last night", circle "Frankie is having trouble staying
awake today"   17. Underline "the television was too loud", circle
"Mother went to read in the kitchen"   18. Underline "After the party",
circle "the whole house needed cleaning" 19. Underline "Patricia was
learning the guitar", circle "she decided to enter the talent show" 20.
Underline "the last sentence is finished", circle "you may now rest"

Week 10 Day 4
1. 27 cu. cm   2. 343 cu. cm   3. 216 cu. cm   4. 15.625 cu. cm
5. 97.336 cu. cm.
Science – no answer needed
1. B   2. D   3. F   4. A   5. C   6. E   7. H   8. G   9. J   10. L
11. M   12. I   13. O   14. N   15. K
1. capitol, capital   2. than, then   3. weak, week   4. farther, further
5. past, passed   6. allusion, illusion   7. altar, alter   8. hoarse, horse
9. quite, quiet   10. you're, your

Week 10 Day 5
J. R. R. Tolkien and C. S. Lewis   1. Friends can agree to disagree, and
enjoy each other's Differences   2. The Narnia Tales   3. The Hobbit and
the Lord of the Rings Trilogy   4. Both loved mythology and believed
that myths and legends could communicate deeper truths and values